WEAPON

MAUSER MILITARY RIFLES

NEIL GRANT

Series Editor Martin Pegler

OSPREY PUBLISHING
Bloomsbury Publishing Plc

Kemp House, Chawley Park, Oxford OX2 9PH, UK
1385 Broadway, 5th Floor, New York, NY 10018, USA
29 Earlsfort Terrace, Dublin 2, Ireland

OSPREY is a trademark of Osprey Publishing, a division of
Bloomsbury Publishing Plc – info@ospreypublishing.com

© 2015 Osprey Publishing

First published in Great Britain in 2015 by Osprey Publishing

A CIP catalogue record for this book is available from the British
Library

Print ISBN: 978 1 4728 0594 2
PDF ebook ISBN: 978 1 4728 0595 9
ePub ebook ISBN: 978 1 4728 0596 6

Index by Mark Swift
Typeset in Sabon and Univers
Battlescenes by Peter Dennis
Cutaway artwork by Alan Gilliland
Originated by PDQ Media, Bungay, UK
Printed and bound in India by Replika Press Private Ltd.

21 22 23 24 25   10 9 8 7 6 5

The Woodland Trust
Osprey Publishing supports the Woodland Trust, the UK's leading
woodland conservation charity.

www.ospreypublishing.com
To find out more about our authors and books visit our website.
Here you will find extracts, author interviews, details of
forthcoming events and the option to sign-up for our newsletter.

Dedication

For my mother, Sheila Grant – with love, and in thanks for all the
time she spent reading to me when I was a child.

Acknowledgements

The author and editor would like to thank the staff and trustees
of the Small Arms School Corps Weapons Collection for their
invaluable assistance in the preparation of this book.

Editor's note

For ease of comparison please refer to the following conversion
table:

1km = 0.62 miles
1m = 1.09yd
1m = 3.28ft
1m = 39.37in
1cm = 0.39in
1mm = 0.04in
1kg = 2.20lb
1g = 0.04oz
1g = 15.43 grains

Cover photographs. Above: a Gew 98. (Author's photograph,
© Royal Armouries PR.612) Below: this soldier has tied his skis
together to create an improvised shooting rest for his Kar 98k.
(Tom Laemlein/Armor Plate Press)

Title-page photograph: An SS sniper on the Eastern Front, with a
4× telescopic sight mounted on his Kar 98k. (Cody Images)

Imperial War Museum Collections

Many of the photos in this book come from the Imperial War
Museum's huge collections which cover all aspects of conflict
involving Britain and the Commonwealth since the start of the
twentieth century. These rich resources are available online to
search, browse and buy at www.iwmcollections.org.uk. In
addition to Collections Online, you can visit the Visitor Rooms
where you can explore over 8 million photographs, thousands of
hours of moving images, the largest sound archive of its kind in
the world, thousands of diaries and letters written by people in
wartime, and a huge reference library. To make an appointment,
call (020) 7416 5320, or e-mail mail@iwm.org.uk
Imperial War Museum www.iwm.org.uk

Artist's note

Readers may care to note that the original paintings from which
the battlescenes in this book were prepared are available for
private sale. All reproduction copyright whatsoever is retained by
the Publishers. All enquiries should be addressed to:

Peter Dennis, 'Fieldhead', The Park, Mansfield, Nottinghamshire
NG18 2AT, UK, or email magie.h@ntlworld.com

The Publishers regret that they can enter into no correspondence
upon this matter.

CONTENTS

INTRODUCTION

When Wilhelm I of Prussia was proclaimed as the first Kaiser (Emperor) of the newly united German Empire in the Hall of Mirrors at Versailles in January 1871, it represented a triumph for the *Realpolitik* of his Chancellor, Otto von Bismarck. Victory in the Franco-Prussian War of 1870–71 had been a precondition for German unification, both to prevent French interference and to increase Prussian prestige as the 'protector' of the smaller German states. However, the German annexation of the French provinces of Alsace and Lorraine (against Bismarck's advice) meant that the French always regarded their defeat as something to be reversed, when possible. France thus allied itself with Russia, forcing Germany to fight on two fronts in any future war. Bismarck was able to prevent political tensions boiling over into war while he retained power, but ultimately the escalation of a crisis in the Balkans in 1914 resulted in Germany launching a pre-emptive attack on France. Germany's hope, embodied in the so-called Schlieffen Plan, was to knock France out of the war quickly before Russia could mobilize, thereby allowing Germany to deal with its enemies one at a time. The failure of this plan, and the harsh peace terms imposed on Germany after its defeat in World War I (1914–18) ultimately led to the rise of the Nazi Party and to World War II (1939–45).

Less directly, success in the Franco-Prussian War also led to the Mauser series of rifles, probably the most important, widely produced and influential 'family' of rifles during the first half of the 20th century. German soldiers went into the Franco-Prussian War armed with the Dreyse 'needle gun', a revolutionary weapon when it was introduced three decades previously. By 1870, however, the Dreyse was a dated design and clearly outclassed by the more modern French Chassepot rifle; the German victory was due to superior strategy, rather than better equipment. The German Army could not permit continued French superiority in small arms, and looked for a weapon as good as the Chassepot, or preferably better. They found it in the designs of the Mauser brothers, and for the next 75 years the primary weapon of almost every German infantryman was a Mauser-designed rifle.

The early black-powder Mauser rifles saw relatively little use in battle, but they evolved into the classic Gew 98 (Gewehr 98, or 'rifle 98') of World War I, and its World War II successor, the Kar 98k (Karabiner 98 kurz, or 'carbine 98 short'). Both were produced in vast numbers and served as the main rifles of the German Army through the two greatest conflicts in its history. The tactical environment changed significantly during this period. New weapons appeared to supplement the rifle, including machine guns, which increasingly became the core of the infantry squad's firepower, with riflemen reduced to carrying ammunition and providing local security. Despite the evolutionary improvements in the Mauser rifle, it was beginning to show its age by World War II. While it could still hold its own against other bolt-action designs, it was outclassed by newer Soviet and American self-loaders. The Germans' efforts to produce their own semi-automatic rifles (the Gew 41 and Gew 43) never met expectations. They persevered, developing the radical MP 44, the first practical assault rifle. The Germans were never able to produce enough of these weapons, however, and the Kar 98k remained in full production until the end of the war.

Had it only been the primary weapon of the German Empire and the Third Reich, the Mauser rifle would still have been an important and influential firearm. In fact, unlike its rivals such as the French Lebel or British Lee-Enfield (which achieved few sales beyond the Empire), Mauser

A wartime German propaganda photo of a soldier with a Kar 98k. Millions of Mauser rifles were produced to arm the German forces in both world wars. (Cody Images)

The long barrel of the Gew 98 is obvious in this picture of German infantry marching up to the line in June 1917. In 1914, carrying rifles around the neck in this manner had been prohibited as 'unsoldierly'. (Tom Laemlein/ Armor Plate Press)

rifles armed much of the world for half a century. Spain, Scandinavian countries and most of Eastern Europe either bought Mauser rifles or manufactured copies themselves, sometimes on original German tooling received as war reparations. Most South and Central American countries purchased Mausers, as did Turkey, Persia and Japan. China received or manufactured so many that 'Mauser' actually became a Chinese word for 'rifle'. Even the United States adopted what was effectively a Mauser clone, the M1903 Springfield. Some of these weapons saw use in the hands of Boers fighting the British in South Africa (1899–1902), in the Spanish–American War of 1898, by Irish Republicans in the Easter Rising of 1916 or with Chinese forces during the 'Warlord Era' of the early 20th century.

Some of the millions produced continued in use after World War II; the Mauser was the standard rifle of the new State of Israel in the 1948 war, while Chinese-made examples were used against UN forces in the Korean War (1950–53). Others were rebarrelled to new calibres (often US .30-06 or 7.62mm NATO) and served on as second-line weapons. The last military examples served as sniping weapons as late as the Yugoslav wars of the 1990s, but hundreds of thousands remain in use to the present day as hunting and sporting rifles. Throughout more than a century of service, the Mauser rifle has established a reputation as an accurate, hard-hitting and reliable weapon, and it remains the classic bolt-action rifle for many people.

DEVELOPMENT
Forging a legend

GERMAN RIFLES BEFORE 1871

The 'needle gun'

Until the 1840s, infantry muskets remained essentially unchanged from the smoothbore weapons of the Napoleonic period. The advantages offered by rifled weapons – much greater accuracy and increased effective range – were well understood, but forcing a ball down the grooves of a rifled barrel took much longer than with a smoothbore, and the tactics of the time valued volume of fire over accuracy. The solution eventually adopted by most European armies was the Minié ball. This was an elongated bullet with a conical hollow in the base. It was small enough to drop down the bore without needing to be forced through the rifling, so the weapon could be loaded as fast as a smoothbore, but when the powder charge fired, the expanding gas pushed out the skirt surrounding the hollow in the base, so that the skirt engaged with the rifling grooves.

The Prussian Army, however, took a different route by adopting the Dreyse *Zündnadelgewehr*, or 'needle gun', in 1841. This gun was a breech-loader, so pushing a bullet down through the rifling was not an issue. The mechanism also meant the firer could reload without having to stand exposed while he rammed the ball home. Breech-loading had been tried before, notably with the screw-breech Ferguson rifle used in small numbers by the British during the American Revolutionary War (1775–83), but these proved too difficult to produce and too fragile to be adopted generally. The Dreyse used a simple bolt action, which was much more practical to mass produce. It was also the first weapon to use a one-piece cartridge without a separate percussion cap. The needle gun got its name from the very long firing pin, which had to pierce this paper cartridge,

The Dreyse 'needle gun'. Introduced in 1841, the Dreyse was the first general-issue bolt-action rifle, but was a dated design by the time of the Franco-Prussian War. (Author's photograph, © Royal Armouries PR.6431)

penetrate through the gunpowder charge and detonate the percussion cap fixed in a papier-mâché sabot at the base of the bullet.

Although the Dreyse was revolutionary when it appeared in 1841, and did well against Austrian troops armed with muzzle-loaders in the war of 1866, it was showing its age by the time of the Franco-Prussian War, and was clearly outclassed by the French Chassepot M1866. The Dreyse had retained a traditional Napoleonic 'carbine bore' of 15.4mm (.61in). However, while the Chassepot had adopted the basic Dreyse design, it fired a smaller 11mm (.433in) bullet at a significantly higher velocity. The velocity gave a much flatter trajectory, and thus a longer effective range. While superior numbers and strategy allowed the Germans to win despite this handicap, the newly unified Germany obviously needed to regain the technological advantage it had lost. It was at this point that the brothers Paul (1838–1914) and Wilhelm (1834–82) Mauser entered the story.

The Mauser brothers

Peter Paul Mauser (always known as Paul) and his older brother Wilhelm were employed in the Royal Armoury of Württemberg, which was still an independent state before 1871. While working there, Paul had developed several improvements to the standard Dreyse needle gun, such as a modification that cocked the weapon as the bolt was worked. These found little favour, however, since the authorities believed the Dreyse to be good enough as it was. The Austro-Hungarian War Ministry was more impressed with the improvements to the design – and the concepts behind them – but no more inclined to purchase the Dreyse, Austria-Hungary having just finished converting its existing muzzle-loaders into breech-loaders using another system. The Austrians did, however, introduce the Mauser brothers to Samuel Norris, the European agent of the American Remington Arms Company.

Norris believed that the Mauser design could be used to convert the French Chassepot rifle to fire a metallic cartridge, which would have significant advantages over the paper or cardboard cartridges then in use. He persuaded the Mauser brothers to go into partnership with him. Whether the brothers properly understood the contract they signed (written in French, a language neither of them spoke) is debatable, and it gave Norris control of their patents provided he made the agreed annual payments to the brothers. In 1867 Norris and the Mauser brothers moved to the famous Belgian gun-making town of Liège, where in 1867–69 they developed a prototype rifle, the so-called 'Mauser-Norris'. The French authorities were not interested in the design, however, and Norris broke his contract with the Mauser brothers, leaving them in an awkward financial position.

EARLY MAUSER RIFLES

The M1871

In 1869 the Royal Prussian Military Shooting School had been sent an example of the Mauser-Norris, and had been impressed enough to include it in the tests the Prussians were conducting to find a replacement for the Dreyse. The Mauser's main rival was the Werder M1869, a breech-loader based on the Peabody dropping-block action, which had been adopted as a Dreyse replacement by Bavaria in the spring of 1869. Eventually, the Mauser design proved itself superior, though the Prussians insisted on a number of changes, most notably an improved safety. Oddly, it was not fitted with an ejector, and after opening the bolt the rifle had to be tilted sideways to remove the cartridge.

The refined Mauser design was a bolt-action rifle in the same 11mm calibre as the Chassepot, but with a key advantage over the French design: the bullet, propellant and primer were all encased in a rigid brass cartridge case. An extractor had to be incorporated into the bolt to handle this cartridge (the paper cartridge of the Dreyse had been completely consumed, like a caseless round), but the system had several significant advantages. First and simplest, the metallic cartridge case was far less likely to be damaged by handling or being knocked around in ammunition pouches than the paper one, and was significantly more resistant to moisture. Second, the detonation of the propellant expanded the ductile brass case to fill the chamber completely, creating a gas-tight seal and eliminating the problems with gas leakage from the breech that had dogged the Dreyse and Chassepot. (Gas leakage meant that escaping propellant gas vented from the weapon's breech, which was unpleasant

The black-powder Mausers. From the top, the Gew 71 infantry rifle, M1871 *Jägerbüchse*, Kar 71 cavalry carbine, and the Gew 71/84 repeater. Note that the projection below the barrel of the Gew 71/84 is a stacking hook, not a cleaning rod. (Author's photograph, © Royal Armouries PR.6389, PR.6393, PR.6386 & PR.6397)

and disconcerting for the user.) Third, the rigid case meant that the primer could be installed at the rear of the case, so that the long and vulnerable needle required to penetrate through the propellant and strike the percussion cap set into the rear of the bullet could be replaced with a much shorter firing pin, removing a weak point in the previous design. Finally, the brass cartridge case absorbed most of the heat of firing, which was then expelled along with the spent cartridge. This meant that the chamber of the rifle took much longer to heat up during sustained firing, and made cook-offs (where the heat of the chamber spontaneously detonated the next round) much less likely.

With its success in the trials, the Mauser design was adopted by the Prussian War Ministry as the Gew 71, though since the individual German states kept control of their own procurement, it did not finally replace the Bavarian Werder until 1877. The Kar 71, a short carbine version of the Gew 71, was developed for cavalry, and for troops whose duties prevented them carrying a full-size rifle, but who needed a weapon to protect themselves. Apart from the short barrel, the straight bolt handle of the rifle was turned downward in the carbine, which also had wood furniture right to the blunt muzzle cap, and no provision for a cleaning rod or bayonet. Although it would accept the standard cartridge, the flash and muzzle blast from the short barrel was excessive, and a special version of the cartridge with a reduced powder charge was issued. Since production of the carbine did not begin until the infantry had been re-equipped with new rifles, the first carbines were not issued until 1876. In the interim, many German cavalrymen were equipped with carbines made from cut-down French Chassepot rifles, large numbers of which had been captured in 1870–71 and adapted for the German cartridge.

A separate version was developed for the *Jäger*, elite skirmishing light infantry and marksmen, similar to the British 'Rifle' regiments. Traditionally, they had been armed with short rifles, rather than the smoothbore muskets of the infantry. The distinction blurred as line infantry gained rifled weapons, but a special *Jäger* version of the Dreyse had been produced, with double set triggers to improve accuracy. Standard military triggers had a relatively heavy trigger pull for safety reasons, but this created muscular tension in the firer's arm, affecting accuracy. With a double trigger, squeezing the first trigger took up the slack in the second trigger, so that it then fired the weapon with a very light trigger pull. The M1871 *Jägerbüchse* was simply a slightly (10cm) shortened version of the standard rifle, with repositioned sling swivels and a special trigger guard with finger grooves. Since it lacked any major advantage over the standard rifle, it would be the last of the special *Jäger* rifles.

The Gew 71/84 repeater

The Gew 71 was a sound design, but it was a single-shot weapon. Paul Mauser tried various methods to add a magazine to it, including tube and box designs, and a U-shape version that wrapped around the receiver. Eventually, he settled on an eight-round tubular magazine that ran beneath the barrel. The new design incorporated other improvements, including an ejector, and was adopted in 1884 as the Gew 71/84. Since the cartridges sat nose-to-tail in the magazine, the bullet was modified by flattening the tip and recessing the primer more deeply, to prevent the nose of one cartridge setting off the primer of the round ahead, although the older round-nosed cartridges could still be used.

Despite the advantages of the Gew 71/84's magazine, it was not in front-line service long before being overtaken by another advance in technology. In 1884, the French chemist Paul Vieille invented 'Poudre B' – called *Poudre Blanche* ('white powder') to distinguish it from standard 'black powder' – the first successful smokeless powder. Conventional gunpowder was technically a 'low explosive' of limited power. It was useless if it became damp and it produced large amounts of smoke, obscuring the firer's view and making his position obvious. By contrast, the new powder was a stabilized form of the high-explosive nitrocellulose. It produced almost three times as much power as the same weight of black powder, was much less sensitive to moisture and produced almost no smoke. 'Poudre B' revolutionized small-arms design. The higher muzzle

This photograph from World War I shows German infantrymen equipped with Gew 88 rifles, easily identified by their sheet-metal barrel shrouds. Although outdated, the Gew 88 was issued in large numbers early in the war, to make good shortages. The men carry the old-fashioned rectangular ammunition pouches, and the man at far left has a disposable ammunition bandolier around his neck, suggesting that these are actually Gew 88/05 or 88/14 conversions, modified to take the new chargers. (Cody Images)

11

velocities it delivered imparted a flatter trajectory, since the shorter flight time to the target meant gravity had less time to act on the bullet, and it was less affected by crosswinds. It became possible to hit targets at much greater ranges, and since the new cartridges contained less propellant, they were lighter and troops could carry more of them. The French quickly fielded the 8mm Lebel M1886 rifle to take advantage of this new technology, and the Gew 71/84 was outclassed within a few years of issue. Because of the very short service life of the Gew 71/84, the prototype cavalry carbine and *Jäger* versions never entered production.

The Gew 88 'Commission Rifle'

The German Army considered simply adapting the existing Gew 71/84 to a smaller-calibre cartridge filled with smokeless powder, but ultimately abandoned the idea in favour of an entirely new weapon. The Gew 88 was developed quickly by the Army's Rifle Testing Commission; despite being Germany's leading rifle designer by this time, Paul Mauser was not involved in the process. The resulting rifle incorporated some elements of previous Mauser designs, particularly in the bolt, but took other features from the Austrian Mannlicher, especially the box magazine. It was chambered for a new 7.92×57mm cartridge, the Patrone 88. This was a bottle-necked 'rimless' design with a groove around the base for the extractor claw, since rimless cartridges fed more smoothly from box magazines than the rimmed British .303in or the sharply tapered French 8mm Lebel. Rounds were loaded into the Gew 88's magazine in a five-round sheet-metal clip, which dropped out of the bottom of the magazine when the last round was chambered. Although this system prevented the magazine being 'topped up' with individual rounds, and the exit slot for the clip created an entry point for dirt, it was still much faster than the Lebel, which featured a tubular magazine like the M71/84 and had to be reloaded one round at a time.

Aware of the advantage the Lebel gave the French, the German Army pushed the Gew 88 into production as quickly as possible; the factories worked around the clock to produce 1.9 million rifles in only two years. This rushed development and testing had inevitable consequences. The Gew 88 was a solid, well-made weapon, and significantly superior to the Lebel. However, it featured a sheet-steel shroud around the barrel. Intended to protect the barrel against knocks and damage, this actually worsened heat build-up during prolonged firing and trapped moisture, causing rust in the barrel beneath. Worse, its rifling design led to very rapid barrel wear, excessive chamber pressure from the new cartridges led to barrel ruptures, and it was possible to load a second cartridge while the first was still unfired in the chamber, leading to breech explosions. All the problems were eventually solved, but not before its shortcomings created a scandal in the press.

A short carbine version, the Kar 88, was produced for cavalry. Like the previous carbine, it featured a side-mounted sling, full-length woodwork, a turned-down bolt handle and a blunt muzzle cap with 'ears' to protect the front sight blade, and it lacked provision for cleaning rod or bayonet.

The almost identical Gew 91 carbine issued to foot artillerymen and specialized units, including airship crews, differed only in the addition of a piling hook at the muzzle to allow it to be stacked.

The Belgian and Spanish Mausers

The Gew 88 'Commission Rifle' has received much abuse from rifle aficionados, partly from its genuine flaws, but also, apparently, simply for not being a Mauser design. It is often suggested that the Commission should have involved Paul Mauser, or waited for him to perfect the design he was already working on. In fact, the commission were probably correct to get a weapon into service as fast as possible; Mauser's next design (the Belgian M1889) did not enter service until 1892, by which time the French Army would have completely re-equipped with the Lebel and enjoyed a significant superiority over the Germans. The 7.65mm M1889 was the first Mauser rifle to use a charger-loading system, where the rounds are slid out of the charger into the magazine, rather than remaining in the clip. It also used an improved bolt design to prevent double loading of cartridges, which had dogged the 'Commission Rifle'. However, it retained the troublesome barrel shroud.

While the Belgian M1889 was not much superior to the 'Commission Rifle', Mauser's next design certainly was. The classic M1893 7mm 'Spanish Mauser' kept the best features of the Belgian model, while discarding the troublesome barrel shroud. The five-round internal magazine was modified to a staggered double-stack design, reducing its depth so it was flush with the stock of the rifle, rather than protruding from the bottom as on previous designs. Apart from the aesthetic appeal of the sleeker lines, this improved the rifle's balance and protected the magazine.

Belgian troops in 1914, armed with M1889 Mausers – note the barrel jackets and protruding magazines. Packed densely into shallow trenches without traverses to stop shrapnel, this firing line would take heavy casualties in an artillery barrage. (Cody Images)

Turkish Mausers

The Turks provided the Mauser company with its first significant order. The Gew 71 and Gew 71/84 rifles for the German Army had been were largely manufactured in government arsenals; Mauser received limited royalties, and was only kept afloat by a contract to produce modified Gew 71 rifles for Serbia. Mauser now developed an improved version of the Gew 71/84 magazine rifle, chambered for a smaller 9.5×60mm round which he believed was the optimal black-powder cartridge. Though Mauser's attempts to interest the British government failed, the Turkish government ordered 500,000 rifles and 50,000 carbines of what became the M87, from its year of introduction.

This huge contract provided several years of work for the Mauser company, and the so-called 'Turkish building' was constructed in a semi-oriental style at the Mauser factory at Oberndorf to accommodate the team of Turkish inspectors working at the site while this contract was under way. The Turks were careful negotiators, and their contract had two important provisions. First, Turkey had to be informed of any rifle improvements patented by Mauser during the contract, and could require these improvements to be incorporated into any rifles still undelivered. Second, if Germany adopted a new rifle during the term of the contract, the Turks could require Mauser to complete the contract with the new German model. Given the timing on the contract, this latter provision could have put Mauser in the awkward position of having to complete the contract with the non-Mauser Gew 88 rifle, but fortunately, the Turks did not exercise that option.

When Mauser developed his first design for a smokeless powder cartridge – the Belgian M1889 – the Turks realized that the M87 had effectively become obsolete, and exercised their contract option. The last 280,000 rifles were thus replaced by an improved version of the M1889 in 7.65×53mm, without the unsatisfactory sheet-metal barrel protector and known as the Turkish Model 1890. The Turks continued to purchase new and improved Mauser designs, buying 200,000 Model 1893 rifles – essentially a version of the Spanish M1893 chambered for the Turkish 7.65mm cartridge. Close military ties to Germany in the run up to World War I meant Turkey adopted a version of the Gew 98 rifle as the Model 1903, initially chambered for the Turkish 7.65×53mm cartridge and later for the standard Mauser 7.92×57mm. Large numbers of these weapons saw service in the various Balkan wars and World War I.

Mauser-armed Turkish troops manning an advanced trench on the Palestine front during World War I. (© IWM Q 56637)

Early experimental models

The German authorities had only regarded the Gew 88 as an interim solution, and began a series of experiments with weapons firing smaller-calibre bullets as early as 1892. The smallest round tested was 5mm, but most of the experiments centred around 6–7.5mm cartridges. Eventually, however, it was decided that the higher velocity and flatter trajectory of the smaller bullets did not offset their reduced lethality at longer range, and the existing 7.92mm cartridge was retained. The early testing was done with modified Gew 88 rifles, while the so called *Kleinkalibriges-Versuchsgewehr* ('Small-Calibre Trials Rifle') Mauser 1896 was used for the later trials. As well as testing the new calibre, this incorporated a number of features that would eventually be found on the Gew 98.

In parallel to this, trials of an upgraded version of the Gew 88 incorporating the improved Mauser bolt action, new sights (named the Lange sight, after its inventor) and a charger-loaded magazine began in 1894, when 200 modified rifles were issued for troop trials, followed by another 2,000 the following year. The Lange sight represented a new design approach, and a rather cleaner and simpler one, using a single curved track to replace the Gew 88 sight, which had required the user to switch between three different rear sight leaves for different ranges. The trials clearly demonstrated the superiority of the Mauser action, and the modified rifle was formally adopted as the Gew 88/97 in March 1897. Plans were made to begin manufacture at the Erfurt arsenal, but the Gew 88/97 never entered full production, and the Gew 98 (a new Mauser design incorporating many of the lessons of the experimental models) was adopted as a German Army standard in April 1898 instead, although Bavaria (which retained independent military procurement) did not follow suit until 1901.

THE Gew 98

The Gew 98 was to become the classic German military rifle, and derivatives remained in service for the next half-century. It retained the flush-fitting staggered magazine of the Spanish M1893, but with a semi-

The Boxer Rebellion in China saw the first use of the Gew 98 in combat. The Kaiser had personally urged troops of the expeditionary force to give no quarter and take no prisoners, instructions gleefully repeated in Allied propaganda during both world wars. (Cody Images)

pistol grip stock, rather than the straight style of previous Mausers. This changed the angle of grip, giving better control of recoil. The action was extremely robust, with a solid receiver rather than the split-bridge receiver of the Gew 88, and a third locking lug on the bolt for maximum strength.

Perhaps most importantly, the clip-loading system of the Gew 88 was replaced by charger loading. After opening the bolt, the user placed the loaded five-round charger into guide rails machined into the receiver, then pressed the cartridges down with his thumb to strip them out of the charger and into the magazine. Since the charger itself never went into the magazine, there was no need to eject it afterwards, which eliminated dirt entry through the clip ejection hole. Magazines could now be topped up with loose rounds, and the chargers themselves were lighter and used less steel than the old clips. Other modifications included a stronger one-piece bolt, new Lange sights and a new method of attaching the bayonet without using a muzzle ring; those fitted to previous models had affected barrel vibration and thus accuracy. Mass production of the new rifle began in 1900, but unlike the Gew 88, complete re-armament was originally expected to take some time; all front-line units were to have the new rifle by 1907, but the Reserve and Landwehr (militia) would not be re-equipped until 1912.

The Gew 98 was designed to fire the existing Patrone 88 cartridge, with its round-nosed bullet. However, the Germans had noted the performance improvement resulting from the pointed French 'Balle D' round introduced for the Lebel in 1898, and began experimenting with a similar bullet themselves. The resulting 'S-Munition' (from *Spitzgeschosse*, or 'Pointed Bullet') was adopted in 1903 and became the new standard round from October 1905. It featured a lighter 9.7g bullet with a better ballistic shape to reduce wind resistance, and an improved propellant, giving a significant increase in muzzle velocity. It fitted the bore more tightly and thus generated higher chamber pressures, especially with the new propellant. The flatter trajectory of the new round necessitated new sights, which were fitted to all new-production rifles, and retrofitted to Gew 98 rifles already issued, and to all Gew 88 weapons remaining in service. A special version (the *Radfahrer-Gewehr*) was produced in small numbers for cyclist detachments, featuring a side-mounted sling for easier carrying across the back, but a full-length barrel and straight bolt handle.

World War I production changes

The Gew 98 saw several changes before the war, including new sights for the S-Munition and small improvements to the bolt and extractor. During the war, receivers were blued or browned rather than receiving the original (and more expensive) polished finish. From 1915, finger grooves were added to the forestock for better grip, and the stamped unit marking plate on the butt was replaced by a perforated disassembly disc on each side of the stock, joined by a hollow washer. This held the firing pin during bolt disassembly and protected it from damage.

Rifle stocks had traditionally been made from walnut, a close-grained wood that was resistant to warping. This was important since a stock that warped in wet or humid conditions would exert pressure on the barrel and thus affect accuracy, but obtaining sufficient seasoned walnut became a problem. Alternative woods such as beech and maple were tried, but proved too prone to warp. Elm proved acceptable, but was not available in sufficient quantities. The problem was worsened by shortage of the linseed oil used to treat the stocks, forcing use of inferior substitutes, including train oil.

Gew 98 carbines

Unlike the British and US armies, who were about to issue new short 'universal rifles' (the Short Magazine Lee-Enfield and Springfield M1903) to all troops, the German Army continued to issue a long rifle (with a 740mm barrel) to infantry and a shorter carbine to cavalry and other troops, such as foot artillerymen. A short-lived Kar 98 was developed to replace the obsolescent Kar 88, featuring a shortened 435mm barrel, a turned-down bolt with flattened, spatulate handle and blunt muzzle cap with 'ears' to protect the front-sight blade when the carbine was in its leather scabbard behind the cavalryman's saddle. It also featured a sling aperture cut through the wooden butt to make the weapon easier to carry across the back, rather than over the shoulder as with the standard rifle sling. However, only a few thousand Kar 98 weapons were made, during a short production run of about 18 months, before it was replaced by the Kar 98A. This was broadly similar, but fitted with an attachment bar for the

World War I-era Mausers. From the top, a Gew 98 with bolt protector and extended magazine, a standard Gew 98, a Kar 98AZ and the unsuccessful pre-war Kar 98. (Author's photograph, © Royal Armouries PR.6414, PR.612, PR.6421 & PR.6417)

Looking rather different from the stereotype of a World War I German soldier, the carbine-equipped hussars manning this boat are patrolling Lake Ochrida on the Macedonian front in 1917. (© IWM Q 86562)

standard rifle bayonet beneath the muzzle. Only about 6,000 were made, since by now the Army was introducing the S-Munition, which produced excessive recoil, flash and muzzle blast when fired from the short barrel.

The solution was to produce a carbine with a longer (590mm) barrel. To save weight, the new weapon was also built around a receiver ring with smaller external diameter (33mm, versus 36mm for the standard Gew 98), a lighter barrel and a slightly altered grip geometry and trigger mechanism, meaning that parts were not interchangeable between carbine and rifle. The bolt handle was still turned downwards, but the spatulate end was replaced by a rounded knob and the cleaning rod was replaced with a piling hook. Initial trials in 1906–07 revealed that the longer barrel made recoil, flash and muzzle blast much more tolerable, but that the design should be modified to take a bayonet. The resulting weapon was adopted in 1908 as the Kar 98AZ (*Aufpflanz- und Zusammensetzvorrichtung*, or 'with bayonet attachment and piling hook'). Well over 1.5 million Kar 98AZ weapons were produced before the end of World War I. As well as cavalrymen, it was also issued to machine-gun and artillery units, and specialist troops such as telegraph units, airship detachments and *Pioniere* (combat engineers). Confusingly, the Kar 98AZ was re-designated the 'Kar 98a' in the inter-war Reichswehr, since none of the original 1902-vintage Kar 98A remained in service.

Finally, a number of Gew 98 rifles were modified into Kar 98b weapons in the 1920s. The latter were carbines only in name, since they retained the original long rifle barrel. The modifications consisted of cutting a slot in the stock for a cavalry-style side-mounted sling, bending down the bolt handle and replacing the sights with a simple design with a minimum range of 100m.

Inter-war Mausers

The Treaty of Versailles at the end of World War I restricted the size of the German Army to 100,000 men, and allowed it to keep only 84,000 rifles and 18,000 carbines, plus another 50,000 rifles for the Reserve. Staff numbers at the Mauser factory plummeted from the peak of 8,000 employed during the war to fewer than 1,000. Many of the company's machine tools were seized or sold, and it diversified into other products to remain in business. Despite the huge number of war-surplus weapons available (many of them obsolete patterns or in poor condition), there was still a market for modern small arms, particularly in China and South America. Both the Czech state arms factory at Brno and the Belgian firm of Fabrique Nationale (FN) were successfully exporting rifles that were essentially short versions of the Gew 98 and even produced on ex-Mauser machinery.

Mauser saw an opportunity to re-enter the military market, and produced a shortened Gew 98 derivative, called the *Standardmodell*, which entered production in a variety of calibres in the mid-1920s. Many were

The German *Sturmtruppen* (assault troops) generally preferred carbines, finding them handier than the long Gew 98. These men carry their Kar 98AZ carbines slung, to leave their hands free to throw the grenades carried in the sandbags under their arms. (Tom Laemlein/Armor Plate Press)

Chinese Mausers

Although records are problematic, the Chinese were very significant users of the Mauser. Their first purchase was the black-powder Gew 71, which saw use against Western forces during the Boxer Rebellion (1899–1901). The Chinese bought considerable numbers of the Gew 88, but their next Mauser purchase was the M1895, almost identical to the influential 7mm Spanish Mauser. This was followed by the M1907 Chinese Mauser, based on the Gew 98, but in 6.8mm. Since the cartridge-case length remained the same, a simple re-barrel could convert it to fire the standard German 7.92mm calibre. The Germans did exactly this with thousands of M1907 rifles awaiting delivery in 1914, which they seized and pressed into their own service. Many more were converted when the Chinese themselves switched to the 7.92mm calibre in the inter-war period, and at least some seem to have been produced in China.

As China fragmented in the 'Warlord Era' of the 1920s, individual commanders purchased a variety of Mauser-copy rifles from Czechoslovakia or FN of Belgium, and indeed, the Kwantung arsenal put copies of these into production themselves, as the Type 21 rifle and carbine. The Nationalist government of General Chiang Kai-shek was initially supported by a German military mission, and bought significant numbers of the Mauser Standardmodell and Kar 98k. When Germany's own re-armament restricted supplies, Madame Chiang visited the Mauser factory personally, and negotiated the purchase of weapons assembled from parts that had failed the very rigorous German inspections, but were still serviceable. After the Japanese invaded China, they applied pressure to their

German ally to stop supplying the Chinese, but by this time the Chinese were manufacturing their own version, as the 'Chiang Kai-Shek' model. Several million (of variable quality) were produced between 1936 and 1949, and saw use against the Japanese and later against Western forces during the Korean War (1950–53).

A Mauser-armed Chinese soldier in July 1945. (Tom Laemlein/ Armor Plate Press)

sold in China and South America, while other examples went to Nazi Germany's Sturmabteilung (SA, or 'Assault Detachment') and Schutzstaffel (SS, or 'Protection Squadron') paramilitary organizations. Since the 740mm barrel of the Gew 98 had proved unwieldy in the trenches, the new weapon featured a 600mm barrel, just slightly longer than that of the Kar 98AZ, but with a standard-weight barrel. The retrospective change to the S-Munition meant the minimum range for the sights of the old Gew 98 was 400m, much too long for trench combat, as shots at closer range went high, and they could only be adjusted in relatively coarse increments of 100m. They were replaced by a new design, which was adjustable in 50m increments, from 100m to 2,000m. This new sight had been carefully designed with a detachable curved rear ramp, which was interchangeable with an alternative ramp calibrated for the sS-Patrone (*schweres Spitzgeschosse*, or 'heavy pointed bullet'); this had been introduced for machine guns in 1918, but being able to use the same round in infantry rifles would offer obvious logistic advantages. The interchangeable ramp allowed the same rifle to be sold to export customers who were still using the older cartridge, or to the German Army, which wanted to standardize on the sS-Patrone. Otherwise, the *Standardmodell* retained the straight bolt handle and bottom-mounted sling of the Gew 98, rather than the turned-down bolt and side-mounted sling of the Kar 98AZ.

To avoid the restrictions on military weapon production imposed by the Allied Military Control Commission, Mauser acquired a Swiss subsidiary in 1931. When Adolf Hitler gained power as German Chancellor in March 1933, he began a programme of covert rearmament almost immediately, and the Mauser company formed an important part of this plan. In late 1933, Mauser introduced a new version of the *Standardmodell*. It is usually termed the 'Mauser Banner' from the logo stamped on the receiver ring, but was identified in company documents as being for the Deutsche Reichspost (German State Post Office), and the rifles themselves were stamped as 'DRP'. While the Post Office did employ armed guards to protect valuable shipments in the troubled Germany of the 1920s and 1930s, the name was simply a camouflage and the expected purchasers were the armed paramilitary organizations of the Nazi Party, such as the SA. However, the Army, anxious to preserve its status as the sole armed force of the state, actually purchased Mauser's entire production run to keep them out of the SA's hands, though some were later passed to the Customs Service and security staff on the state railway system.

The main differences from the *Standardmodell* were that the bolt handle was turned down for easier carriage and the stock recessed below it, and a slot was cut into the butt for a carbine-style side-mounted sling.

THE Kar 98k

In 1934, the Heereswaffenamt ('Army Weapons Office') issued a requirement for a new rifle, to be used by all three armed services (i.e. the Army, Navy and Air Force). The specification closely followed that of the DRP rifle, including the turned-down bolt handle, though a hold-open device was added to the bolt. Both Mauser and J.P. Sauer & Sohn (who had manufactured the Gew 98 during World War I) tendered, but the two prototypes were almost identical; the main difference was that the Sauer prototype used a different method of retaining the barrel bands. The new

The muzzle of an early Kar 98k. The barrel band is still carefully machined into an H-shape to reduce weight, and it has the detachable sheet-metal front-sight protector and muzzle cover in place. As the war went on, the barrel band became cruder, to save production time, and the sight protector was replaced by a fixed sight hood and semi-disposable muzzle plugs. (Author's photograph, © Royal Armouries PR.11783)

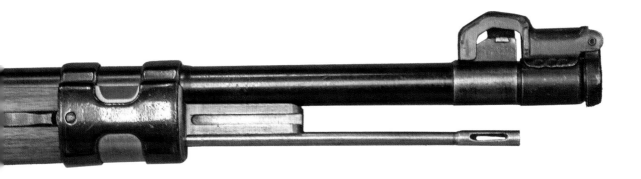

World War II-era Mausers. From the top, the 1924 *Standardmodell*, the DRP rifle, the Kar 98k, the Gew 33/40 carbine and the last-ditch VK 98. (Author's photograph, © Royal Armouries PR.6432, PR.10678, PR.11783, PR.6309 & PR.6447)

rifle was officially adopted as the Kar 98k (from the German *kurz*, or 'short') in June 1935 and went into production at both Mauser and Sauer factories, the latter switching over to use Mauser-style barrel bands.

Although officially designated a carbine, the Kar 98k was actually a similar length to the short 'universal rifles' adopted by the British and Americans. It was intended for issue to all troops, replacing both rifle and carbine. The adoption of the Kar 98k coincided with Hitler's repudiation of the limitations the Versailles Treaty imposed on Germany's armed forces, and the re-introduction of conscription. This huge expansion of the Army meant that the demand for the new rifle far exceeded supply, and additional manufacturers were brought into the programme as quickly as possible. To help cover the shortage, some old Gew 98 and Kar 98b rifles were converted into Kar 98k weapons; this involved shortening the barrels and re-working or replacing the wooden stocks to match, replacing the sights, plus – for the Gew 98 – bending down the bolt handle and cutting a slot in the stock to attach the carbine-type sling. The original markings were usually left unchanged, and new proof marks added.

A World War II German soldier aiming his Kar 98k. Note how the textbook kneeling position shown here supports the left elbow, for a more stable aim. (Tom Laemlein/ Armor Plate Press)

Wartime changes

Although the Kar 98k remained in service throughout World War II, various small changes were made during that time, mostly to simplify production. Shortage of walnut for stocks became a problem again from 1937. The solution adopted was to make the stocks from laminated beechwood, which did not warp significantly. These were actually stronger than the solid walnut stocks, although 200–300g heavier. Laminated stocks were used for the vast majority of rifles manufactured after 1938. Woodwork on early models sometimes cracked or broke near the muzzle. This fault was addressed by placing the cleaning-rod holder deeper into the stock; this also necessitated lengthening the cleaning rod, from 250mm to 320mm.

From December 1939, new rifles were fitted with a permanently attached hood to protect the front-sight blade from damage, and a new buttplate with built-up side walls was introduced. Commonly referred to as the 'cupped' buttplate, this gave the edges of the butt better protection than the previous flat buttplate. The steel band holding the forestock together had originally been machined into a 'H' shape to reduce weight and was pinned in place, but from 1942 this was progressively replaced by a solid band without the weight-reducing machining, and ultimately by a simpler stamped and welded band.

By 1943, the duplicate range settings on the underside of the rear sight were omitted. Mauser began experimenting with using stampings to replace the machined parts in the trigger guard and magazine assembles. Despite difficulties in producing stamped parts to sufficiently close tolerances, other manufacturers followed suit or bought stamped parts from Mauser. By late 1944, the oval gas-escape holes in the bolt were replaced by simpler round drilled ones, bluing of the metal parts to prevent corrosion had been replaced by cruder phosphating and the wooden stocks were less carefully finished, especially on the outside surface. The serial numbering of minor parts was also discontinued,

THE MAUSER EXPOSED

7.92×57mm Kar 98k

1. Front sight
2. Upper barrel band
3. Lower band barrel with front sling attachment
4. Handguard
5. Rear sight
6. Receiver
7. Bolt handle
8. Bolt sleeve
9. Safety catch
10. Cocking piece
11. Buttstock

12. Buttplate (flat type)
13. Buttplate retaining screws
14. Disassembly disc
15. Rear sling slot
16. Trigger
17. Trigger guard
18. Cartridges
19. Stock
20. Bayonet mount
21. Cleaning rod
22. Barrel

23. Chamber
24. Firing pin
25. Firing-pin spring
26. Rear retaining screw
27. Sear
28. Sear spring
29. Floorplate latch and spring
30. Magazine spring
31. Magazine follower
32. Floorplate
33. Front retaining screw

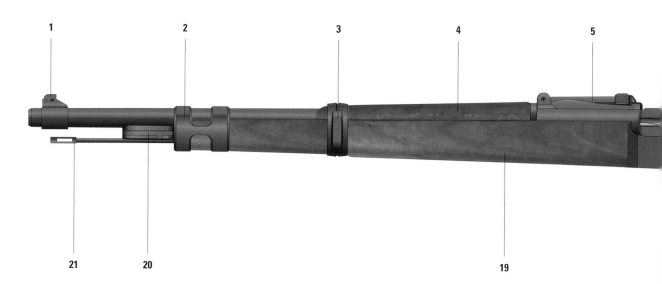

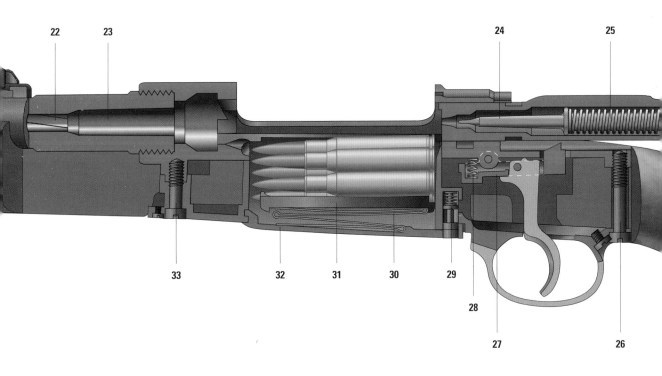

22 23 24 25

33 32 31 30 29

28

27 26

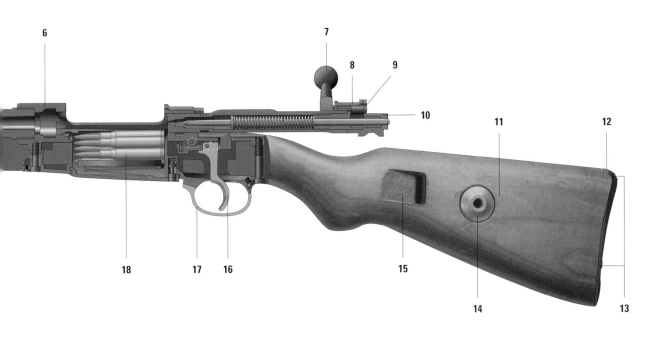

6 7 8 9

10

11 12

18 17 16 15 14 13

except on weapons to be fitted with telescopic sights, and milling marks were no longer carefully polished off the receivers.

Not all manufacturers introduced the changes at the same time, and since manufacturers bought parts from a number of different subcontractors and used old stocks of parts to complete rifles, some surviving weapons can demonstrate a mix of these features.

The *Kriegsmodell*

Proposals for a 'Kar 98v' (*vereinfachung*, or 'simplified') were first put forward in late 1943. While some of the recommendations were adopted and are included above, others (notably deletion of the bayonet lug, cleaning rod and bolt disassembly disc) were not. As Germany's position worsened, many of the rejected suggestions were implemented. The bayonet lug and cleaning rod were replaced by a simple end cap, while the disassembly disc was replaced by a simple hole drilled in the side of the buttplate. Barrel bands were further simplified or even replaced with wood screws. Stocks were now only roughly finished, without sanding, and were no longer stained or varnished to prevent their absorbing moisture. These simplifications were incorporated into examples produced at some plants from late 1944, and such weapons are commonly known by collectors as the *Kriegsmodell* version. However, neither this nor the 'Kar 98v' nomenclature was formally adopted to distinguish such weapons. A few were even fitted with a simple fixed sheet-metal rear sight; it was only marked to 500m, but the days of long-range shooting were past, and it saved nearly an hour of production time.

Germany's last-ditch rifle – the VK 98

By 1945, with the Nazi Reich tottering under assaults from both East and West, desperate attempts to produce more weapons for the *Volkssturm* militia saw a number of designs for new weapons, many of them simple to the point of crudity. The VK 98 (*Volks-Karabiner*, or 'people's carbine') was based on the Kar 98k, but stripped of everything but the absolute essentials. Examples vary, but most have simple half-stocks that provide a minimal handgrip while leaving most of the barrel exposed, and very simple stamped sights. All have very crude machining and stocks roughed out of wood blanks. This weapon is sometimes referred to as the VG 1 (*Volksgewehr*, or 'People's Rifle'), although the same designation is also used for other weapons based on drastically simplified versions of the MP 44 assault rifle.

The VK 98's action was that of a Kar 98k, but the finish was extremely crude and the sights were simply stamped from sheet metal. Some used parts salvaged from damaged weapons or previously rejected for not meeting quality standards. (Author's photograph, © Royal Armouries PR.6447)

MAUSER WEAPONS IN CONTEXT

Weapon*	Calibre	Barrel length	Overall length	Unloaded weight**	Magazine
M1871 (Germany, 1871)	11×60mm	855mm	1,345mm	4.5kg	Single
M71/84 (Germany, 1884)	11×60mm	800mm	1,300mm	4.6kg	8-rd tubular
Lebel 1886 (France, 1886)	8×50mm	800mm	1,300mm	4.2kg	8-rd tubular
Gew 88 (Germany, 1888)	7.92×57mm	740mm	1,245mm	3.9kg	5-rd clip
Gew 98 (Germany, 1898)	7.92×57mm	740mm	1,250mm	4.1kg	5-rd charger
Kar 98 (Germany, 1900)	7.92×57mm	435mm	945mm	3.3kg	5-rd charger
Kar 98AZ (Germany, 1908)	7.92×57mm	590mm	1,090mm	3.8kg	5-rd charger
Kar 98k (Germany, 1934)	7.92×57mm	600mm	1,110mm	4.1kg	5-rd charger
M1 Garand (USA, 1936)	.30-06 (7.62×63mm)	610mm	1,103mm	4.4kg	8-rd clip
Gew 33/40 (Germany, 1940)	7.92×57mm	490mm	990mm	3.8kg	5-rd charger
Lee-Enfield No. 4 (Britain, 1941)	.303in (7.7×56mm)	640mm	1,129mm	4.1kg	10-rd charger
Gew 41 (M) (Germany, 1941)	7.92×57mm	550mm	1,172mm	5.0kg	10-rd charger
Gew 43 (Germany, 1943)	7.92×57mm	558mm	1,117mm	4.3kg	10-rd box

*All the weapons in the table are bolt-action, except the Gew 41 (M), Gew 43 and M1 Garand, which are semi-automatic.

**Weights may vary slightly between examples of the same weapon, e.g. because some versions have less surplus metal machined away to save weight in order to speed production, and Kar 98k weapons with laminated stocks are slightly heavier.

THE MAUSER RIFLES THAT NEVER WERE

Some Mauser prototypes never came to fruition. The Gew 98/17 was to have been a Gew 98 modified for trench fighting, with a modified barrel profile, a bolt hold-open similar to that fitted to the Kar 98k, sights with a shorter 100m minimum range, a ribbed trigger to prevent the firer's finger slipping in muddy conditions and an improved bolt protector that did not hamper charger loading. The Mauser 'Trench & Close Combat Rifle 1918' was a private development, with a similar improved bolt protector and hold-open device, an improved stock shape and a revised cocking and firing mechanism. More importantly, it did away with charger loading in place of detachable box magazines, of five-, ten- or 25-round capacity. Few were produced, but it reappeared after World War I as the Mauser Militär-Gewehr 1929, slightly amended to feature the interchangeable ramp sights of the *Standardmodell*.

World War II threw up a number of one-off developments, including test rifles with plastic furniture instead of wood, and a prototype chambered for the 7.92×33mm round of the MP 44. Perhaps the most interesting is the Gew 40k, effectively a slightly modified Kar 98k with a barrel shortened to 490mm. It never went beyond prototype stage, and presumably would have suffered the same problems of flash and recoil as the earlier short carbines.

USE
Facing the test of battle

OPERATION AND MAINTENANCE

Firing the Mauser

The Mauser 98-series rifles all operated similarly. To load, the user opened
the bolt and positioned a five-round charger in the guide slot machined
into the receiver bridge. He then used a thumb to push the cartridges
down out of the charger and into the magazine. Pushing the bolt forward
automatically knocked the empty charger aside.

Gravity and air resistance mean that bullets actually travel in a
parabola, rather than a straight line. Soldiers were therefore taught how
to estimate range during their basic training, and the back sight was
adjusted by sliding it along its track to the appropriate range mark to
compensate for this curved path. With the sights adjusted, the firer aimed
by centring the post of the front sight between the two upright arms of the
back sight.

The safety catch is a three-position 'wing' at the rear of the bolt.
Turned to the right, it locks both bolt and firing pin to make the weapon
safe. Turning it to the left permits the weapon to fire, while the upright
middle position locks the firing pin but not the bolt, for loading and
unloading. Recoil is typical for the military rifles of the period, with their
full-power cartridges, i.e. noticeable but controllable with a decent firing
stance. Troops sometimes complained of bruising from recoil after firing
40–50 rounds in a reasonably short period. Recoil with the very short-
barrelled variants was notably more severe, making them actively
unpleasant to fire. Firing noise exceeded 160dB, enough to cause some
hearing damage for soldiers firing the weapon regularly without ear
protection. For soldiers fighting in the trenches of the Western Front or

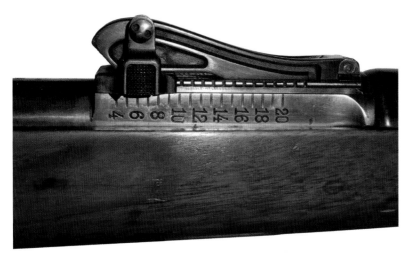

The Lange sight fitted to the Gew 98. Sliding the pin along the track to the correct range mark raised the sight, to compensate for bullet drop at longer ranges. This is the later version with the amended curve for the S-Munition; note the extremely long minimum range of 400m. The Lange sight was replaced by a simpler tangent sight using the same principles on the Kar 98k. (Author)

the rubble of Stalingrad, this was unlikely to be their most pressing concern, however.

To chamber the next cartridge after firing, the right hand pushed the bolt knob up to unlock the bolt, then pulled it rearward to eject the spent case. Pushing the bolt forward again and down to lock it chambered the next round, and the rifle was ready to fire again. Soldiers were generally taught to use the edge or palm of the hand to manipulate the bolt rather than the fingers, since this could be done more easily wearing winter gloves, and more force could be applied when dealing with a fouled weapon. In extreme cases, the bolt of an overheated or heavily fouled weapon could be kicked open with a boot heel.

The Gew 98 bolt would close on an empty chamber, but a hold-open device was added in the Kar 98k. After the last round had been fired, the top edge of the magazine follower caught the bolt and prevented it being pushed forward, warning the firer he needed to reload. To close the bolt without reloading, the follower had to be depressed with a finger.

The author with a World War I-era Kar 98AZ carbine during a vintage rifle shoot at Bisley. Although almost a century old, both versions of the Gew 98 and the Kar 98AZ he fired still shot perfectly. The Mauser excelled at range shooting, and even a thoroughly indifferent shot like the author was easily able to rack up consistent head and heart shots at 200m, the likely World War I battle range. The longer barrel of the Gew 98 was slightly more accurate firing prone supported, but the author actually found the lighter carbine easier from a standing position, where the rifle's long barrel tended to magnify any muzzle shake. This sort of shooting obviously represents optimal conditions; the adrenalin and fear experienced on the 'two-way range' of the battlefield does little for shooting accuracy, and much to explain the very high numbers of rifle rounds fired to inflict relatively small numbers of casualties. The sights were adequate, though perhaps not visible enough in poor light. Recoil was entirely controllable, though the author did (embarrassingly) receive a small pressure cut above his right eye from the telescopic sight when he didn't leave quite enough eye relief on his first shot with a sniper version of the Gew 98. (Author)

Training in the Kaiser's army

Using his weapon effectively is the key ability of a soldier, and in the years before World War I, the Kaiser's army had a structured programme of training to ensure that the recruit was capable of doing so. Since the Army needed to train large numbers of short-service conscripts, the training method differed from those used with long-service regulars, such as those of the pre-war British Army. Training began with drill and learning to load and unload the weapon with inert practice cartridges before moving to the firing range, where each soldier fired at a number of target series in several positions (prone, kneeling and standing) at known ranges up to 400m.

The aim was not to teach each soldier to shoot as well as possible, but to ensure he met the specified standard, which was higher for soldiers in the second year of their two-year enlistment. As a result, the annual ammunition allocation for training (24,825–28,800 rounds for an infantry company, depending on manpower) was pooled, and poor shots actually received more practice than good shots, until they reached the required standards. Marksmanship awards, usually in the form of decorative lanyards, were awarded to soldiers who achieved the required score on each exercise using the lowest number of rounds, rather than for achieving the highest number of hits with a set number of rounds. *Jäger* and the similar *Schützen* units had to meet higher standards of marksmanship and consequently received twice the ammunition allocation for training, while other branches had lower standards and received a lower ammunition allocation.

Once the soldiers had achieved a basic standard of marksmanship on the range, firing was integrated into large-scale field exercises, with the entire platoon or company firing on targets. Scores in this phase were assessed for the unit as a whole, rather than individuals, and the exercises put stress on training officers and NCOs to control and direct the unit's fire, as well as the soldiers' ability to hit the target. Range estimation was also important, since the targets were generally not at known distances, and a number of soldiers in each company received extra training as 'range finders' for their comrades. Even after the standard rifle was re-sighted for the new S-Munition in 1905, marksmanship training continued to be done with the old Patrone 88 for years afterwards, until the entire existing stock of 160 million old-style cartridges had been used up! Despite this, when recalling his training the veteran Stephen Westman still felt that 'Our training ... was centred on firing on the rifle ranges, and I must say that after a few weeks our instructors succeeded in making almost every one of us a first class shot' (Westman 1968: 30).

Under the pressures of World War I, recruit training was compressed to get men to the front as quickly as possible. By 1918 the number of exercises each soldier had to fire to achieve the standard was reduced by eliminating those exercises seen as less relevant, though the scores required for the remaining exercises stayed the same. All the combatant powers suffered from a declining standard of marksmanship among their troops as the war dragged on. If anything, the Germans suffered this less than most, owing to their pre-war emphasis upon training large numbers of reservists to a reasonable standard, rather than creating smaller numbers of high-quality marksmen. No German unit could have matched the much-vaunted

On the firing range. Note the wooden 'shooting table' the recruit is lying on; these were standard at German firing ranges. (Cody Images)

musketry of the British Army of 1914, but very few of those British pre-war regulars were left in the ranks by 1916. By contrast, most German units retained a solid number of men with pre-war training into 1917 and sometimes later. Even so, by spring 1918 Hauptmann Walter Bloem of Grenadier-Regiment 12 was lamenting that 'The Grenadiers of 1918 do not shoot like those of 1914, especially at long ranges. Practically all they know about is fighting in trenches' (quoted in Pegler 2004: 151).

Training in the Wehrmacht

Until 1935, the size of the Reichswehr was limited by the Treaty of Versailles to 100,000 men, each enlisting for a minimum of 12 years. It thus had both time to train every recruit extremely thoroughly, and incentive to do so, to create a cadre for a much larger force, if and when the army expanded beyond the Versailles limitations. Even once conscription was introduced in 1935, the newly renamed Wehrmacht continued to give recruits 16 weeks of basic training, significantly longer than any of its adversaries. Many Wehrmacht recruits also arrived with a higher level of knowledge than their equivalents in other countries, from paramilitary experience in the Hitlerjugend ('Hitler Youth', compulsory from 1936 for boys of 14 and older) or from their compulsory stint with the Reichsarbeitsdienst (RAD, or 'State Labour Service'), which included things such as military courtesies and foot drill (with shovels substituting for rifles) in its training. Trainee *Fallschirmjäger* (paratrooper) Martin Pöppel found this prior experience very helpful:

> My best skills were in shooting. I already had a head start here because I'd been something of a marksman during my days in the Hitler Youth, so I soon got a little bit of special leave to compensate me for a few punishment drills. In the hundred metres prone I scored 34 out of 36 possible rings in the silhouette target. (Pöppel 2008: 11)

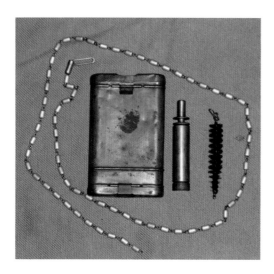

The Reiningungsgerät 34 cleaning kit, with chain pull-through, oil bottle and chamber brush. Unfortunately, the bore brush and take-down tool are missing from this example. The kits were originally well made, but quality declined through the war years. (Author)

During initial drill and handling, the recruits learned to load their rifles wearing gas masks or in the dark, as well as under range conditions. Marksmanship was integrated with field training so far as possible, including in mock-ups of complete Russian villages. The majority of marksmanship training still took place on the firing range, however, though Allied officers inspecting these ranges after the war often commented favourably on the quality and sophistication of their equipment. A small-bore .22in *Kleinkaliber Wehrsportgewehr* ('Small Calibre Military and Sporting Rifle'), deliberately designed so that its weight, sights and safety controls were almost identical to those of the service rifle, was used by shooting clubs and the Hitlerjugend, and to allow military training where a full-sized range was not available.

The German shooting manual covered marksmanship fairly solidly, and included rather more firing positions than other countries' manuals, including several seated positions and some positions of dubious utility, like shooting from a tree. Much of the marksmanship training emphasized relatively short ranges (less than 300m), as most engagements took place at these ranges, and longer-range fire was delivered using machine guns where possible. Thanks to the Wehrmacht's emphasis on the machine gun as the core of squad firepower, the recruits with the best marksmanship scores were generally assigned as machine-gunners, rather than becoming riflemen. As in World War I, mounting casualties put pressure on recruit training, which was reduced to 12–14 weeks in 1944, though this still compared favourably to US or British levels, let alone Soviet ones. Meanwhile, infantry units were increasingly bulked out by men transferred from the Kriegsmarine (German Navy) and Luftwaffe (German Air Force), who had received basic rifle training with their original service but not proper infantry training.

Caring for the Mauser

The Mauser 98-series weapons were relatively simple, robust and reliable, but still needed a certain amount of care to keep functioning, and looking after his weapon was a fundamental routine learned by a new recruit. The Gew 98 was fitted with a cleaning rod in a tube below the muzzle. However, each rod was of little use on its own; several were screwed together to create a full-length cleaning rod, to which greased oakum was attached to clean the bore.

From 1934, each rifleman was issued an individual cleaning kit, the so-called Reiningungsgerät 34. This was a rectangular tin about the size of a tobacco tin, with hinged flaps covering both ends, and was carried either in the bread bag or in a special pocket of the assault pack. One compartment of the tin contained cleaning patches, while the other contained a chain pull-through to clean the barrel, an oil bottle, a bore brush, a chamber brush and a disassembly tool. It is not clear why a chain (rather than cord) pull-though was used, as it was well known that repeated or careless use of the chain pull-through could easily damage the bore and impair accuracy. Although the issue of this kit meant that the cleaning rod was no longer used for routine cleaning, it continued to be fitted to new rifles almost to the end of the war, as it was useful for pushing split cases out of the barrel.

Early Kar 98k weapons were issued with a sheet-metal front-sight protector/muzzle cover, but this had to be removed before firing the weapon. After the rifle design was modified to include a fixed hood to protect the front sight, soldiers were issued four semi-disposable rubber muzzle plugs to prevent mud and dirt entering the barrel; the rifle could be fired with this plug in place, if necessary.

A standard 7.92×57mm cartridge, alongside the massive 13.2×92mm cartridge of the M1918 anti-tank rifle. (Martin Pegler)

The *Landser*'s load – ammunition carriage

Each rifleman was issued with a pair of ammunition pouches, worn on either side of the waistbelt. Rear-echelon personnel and heavy-weapons crews equipped with carbines for self-defence were sometimes issued only a single ammunition pouch. The ammunition pouch issued for the Gew 88 was the rectangular M95 pattern, which held three 15-round packets (each packet held three five-round clips). NCOs received the smaller M88 pouch, which held two 15-round packets of ammunition, and the support troops such as engineers and artillerymen received a pair of smaller pouches (the M87/88); each pouch held three loose five-round clips.

These rectangular single-compartment pouches were replaced by a design with three separate pouches on the same backing, each with its own fastening, so that only the ammunition in the open compartment could be lost if the soldier dived for cover. The revised triple ammunition pouch was

During World War II, men of 13. Waffen-Gebirgs-Division der SS *Handschar* parade with Kar 98k rifles. The division was raised largely from Bosnian Muslims, and used primarily for anti-partisan operations in Croatia. These personnel wear the standard three-compartment M1911 ammunition pouches, although without the leather shoulder braces usually worn to help support the weight of the belt equipment. (Cody Images)

produced in two versions. Infantrymen received the M1909 pouch, which held four five-round clips in each of its triple pockets, for a total of 60 rounds per pouch. Cavalry were issued the M1911 pouch, identical except that each pocket held only two clips, for a total of 30 rounds per pouch. The triple M1909 and M1911 designs were standard throughout World War I, although the older pouches were still issued to make good shortages in the early years of the war. The same triple pouches remained in service through the Reichswehr period until 1933, when the M1911 pouch was made the standard for all troops. It remained so throughout World War II, though versions holding three clips per compartment were also produced.

In addition to their ammunition pouches, infantrymen carried additional ammunition in their packs, for a total standard load of 150 rounds per man. Despite this allocation, when the Gew 98 was first introduced, there were fears that infantry armed with such 'quick-firing' rifles might expend their ammunition very quickly, leaving themselves defenceless. As a result, rifle ammunition was issued packaged in bandoliers from 1908, so that troops going into action could easily carry extra ammunition. Each bandolier held 14 five-round clips in individual compartments, and the company ammunition wagon held a bandolier (i.e. 70 rounds) for every rifleman in the company as an immediate reserve. Four bandoliers were packed in a cardboard box, with five boxes to each wooden ammunition crate, i.e. 1,400 rounds per crate. Shortages of cotton meant the bandoliers were abandoned from 1917, and each of the five cardboard boxes in each crate then held 20 smaller boxes, each holding three five-round clips, i.e. 1,500 rounds per case.

THE MAUSER IN COMBAT BEFORE 1914

The Spanish–American War of 1898

It is one of the ironies of military history that the Mauser rifle first saw battle as far from its German homeland as it was possible to get. There had been numerous revolts against Spanish rule in its colonial possessions (Cuba, Guam and the Philippines) during the last decades of the 19th century. US public opinion was generally sympathetic to the rebels, especially after severe measures were imposed following the 1895 Cuban revolt. Despite warmongering by the 'yellow press', President McKinley negotiated a peaceful settlement with the Spanish government that would have given Cuba autonomy. However, riots in Havana lead McKinley to dispatch the battleship USS *Maine* to safeguard US citizens in Cuba. When the Spanish were blamed for the mysterious explosion that destroyed *Maine*, war broke out.

The Spanish troops were plentifully armed with Mauser M1893 rifles. The US troops were mostly equipped with the Krag-Jørgensen rifle. Although only adopted in 1894 as the first US rifle to use smokeless powder, the 'Krag' was slower firing, since it was loaded with single rounds rather than the much faster Mauser chargers, and its weaker .30-40 cartridge had a significantly shorter effective range. Ironically, the

US had tested several Mauser rifles of the Belgian M1889 type during the trial that resulted in the adoption of the Krag-Jørgensen; although the Mauser weapons were judged accurate and reliable, the Krag was adopted because of its better performance as a single-shot weapon.

Despite being heavily outnumbered in most engagements, the better-armed Spanish regulars were able to inflict very significant casualties on the US forces. At the battle of San Juan Hill (1 July 1898), 750 Spanish regulars were able to inflict 1,400 casualties on the attacking US troops in a matter of minutes. Without the very heavy fire of the supporting American Gatling gun battery, the assault on the position might even have ended in a US defeat, rather than a costly victory. In the aftermath of the war, the Krag-Jørgensen was swiftly replaced by the M1903 Springfield, a rifle incorporating so many Mauser features that the US government was obliged to pay Mauser royalties for each one produced after he sued for patent infringements.

The 2nd Anglo-Boer War (1899–1902)

Relations between the British Empire (represented in southern Africa by the colonies of Natal and the Cape Colony), and the Boer republics of the Orange Free State and Transvaal had historically been unsettled. After all, the two Afrikaans-speaking republics had actually been created by Boers who had chosen to migrate north rather than live under British rule in the first place, and the two sides had fought a four-month war (the 1st Anglo-Boer War) in 1880–81 over previous British attempts to annex the Transvaal. Tensions were exacerbated by the discovery of vast gold deposits at Witwatersrand, and the consequent influx of immigrant miners to exploit the deposits, largely from Britain and its empire. These 'Uitlanders' were heavily taxed by the Boer governments, and not permitted to vote unless they fulfilled onerous conditions. While the British press viewed this as unreasonable oppression, the Boers saw the Uitlanders as an unwelcome social disruption. Matters were brought to a head by the 'Jameson Raid' in December 1896, an attempted semi-official *coup d'état* in the Transvaal. Although the raid ended in fiasco, and was repudiated by the British government, the two sides were on the road to war.

In preparation, the Transvaal government purchased 37,000 Mauser rifles (similar to the M1893 model supplied to Spain), along with some modern artillery. These weapons

Boer commandos. A posed shot like this is likely to have been taken early in the war, and the Boers are armed with Mauser M1895 rifles and carbine (at left; note the sling attachment, mounted on the side of the butt). Mauser slings were of leather, 30mm wide, though shortages meant that slings issued towards the end of World War I were sometimes of woven canvas, with short leather sections at either end to support the buckle. Carbine slings were shorter and had a different buckle arrangement, as they attached via the slot in the stock. Oddly, these two rifles appear to be missing their cleaning rods. (Cody Images)

became the mainstay of the Boer forces during the early part of the war, supplemented by the privately owned rifles most Boers had brought along when they assembled in their 'Commandos'. Meanwhile, negotiations between the governments reached stalemate. The British demanded full political equality for the Uitlanders while President Kruger demanded the withdrawal of all British troops from the borders of the Transvaal. Since neither side wished to comply with the other's demands, war was declared in October 1899.

Surprisingly, Britain had not reinforced its South African garrisons in the run up to the war, and the first few months saw the Boers on the offensive, invading the Cape Colony and laying siege to a number of towns, including Ladysmith and Mafeking. However, none of the besieged towns was actually captured, and once British reinforcements arrived, they began an offensive to relieve them. Unfortunately for the British, however, many of the Boers had been shooting for the pot since childhood, and shooting events had been a common feature of Boer social life. As a result, many Boers were excellent shots, and armed with the latest weapons, they were able to inflict significant casualties on the British, culminating in a series of British defeats at Stormberg (10 December 1899), Magersfontein (11 December) and Colenso (15 December) in the so called 'Black Week', which stalled the British relief operations on all fronts with heavy casualties.

These British reverses were all attributed to heavy and accurate Boer rifle fire. During the night attack at Magersfontein, for example, the preliminary British artillery barrage failed to suppress the Boer defenders, who had dug their trenches at the base of the hill, rather than on the crests where the British expected them to be. The alerted defenders then engaged

2nd Anglo-Boer War, 1901 (opposite)

Despite suffering severe reverses in the early stage of the 2nd Anglo-Boer War, the British had effectively defeated the organized Boer armies by the end of the first year of conflict. Yet it took another two years to root out the last resistance from small, mobile groups of 'bitter enders' who continued to conduct hit-and-run attacks against British forces, until finally robbed of their mobility by a network of blockhouses and barbed-wire fences. Although many Boers began the war with Mauser 1896 carbines (similar to the Spanish M1893 model) like that carried by the nearest figure, a few were armed with older weapons such as the black-powder Mauser Gew 71 carried by his father, next to him. By the end of the war, however, shortage of Mauser ammunition had forced many to re-equip themselves with captured British Lee-Enfield rifles, as carried by the furthest figure. Although the British regarded use of captured weapons as legitimate, they took a very hard line against Boers replacing their worn-out clothing with elements of uniforms taken from British casualties or prisoners. After several unfortunate incidents where Boers had used captured uniforms to get close to British troops before firing on them, any Boer captured wearing British khaki, such as the trousers worn by the far figure, were routinely shot. Although the British made great efforts to improve the mobility of their forces by mounting infantry, they suffered appalling horse casualties from disease and shortage of water and fodder, leading to experiments with mechanical transport, such as the Fowler armoured traction engine seen here.

the advancing Highland Brigade at about 400m, inflicting 700 casualties (including its commanding general and one of the four battalion commanders) in a matter of minutes before the Highlanders could deploy from the close formation they had adopted to avoid losing cohesion during the night approach march. Dawn saw the remnants of the Highland Brigade's four battalions still pinned down in front of the Boer trenches, where they had to lie for most of the following day, unable to advance or retreat because of the accurate rifle fire and in danger of being encircled by Boer forces working their way round their flanks. The open terrain was almost ideal for the Mauser, as this Boer account shows:

> By the time the foremost infantrymen came within 1,200 yards [1,100m] of us, many fallen dotted the veld, and their advance wavered before the hail of bullets. They did not run away, but we saw them taking cover behind ant-heaps and such other shelter as the ground afforded. From there they directed a heavy fire on us, but their progress was definitely stayed, and our line held for the rest of the day. (Reitz 2010: 29)

Although sources do mention very long-range shooting like this, it is worth remembering that they generally refer to group-firing at groups of men, rather than individuals – at these ranges, a single man would be smaller than the front-sight post. Several high-scoring German snipers, interviewed after World War II, indicated that they rarely expected consistent hits beyond 600–800m, even with telescopic sights (Senich 1982:115).

Another major factor in the Mauser's dominance during the 2nd Anglo-Boer War was the relative limitations of the artillery of the day, which had benefited from the new smokeless powder and improved explosives, but remained essentially a direct-fire weapon and was unable to deliver the sort of barrages that would be used to cover similar assaults during World War I. Things did not always go the Boers' way, however. Although the Mauser rifles had been purchased with bayonets, many Boers had discarded them, while others were using hunting rifles that lacked bayonet lugs. More than one Boer discovered that if one continued to fire on the charging British until they were almost upon you, then dropped the rifle and raised your hands at the last moment, the angry British were not always in a mood to accept the surrender.

The British did not take their defeats well, and dispatched more regular troops, accompanied by large numbers of volunteers from across the Empire. Although the British still suffered significant losses and some unpleasant reverses before they finally relieved the besieged towns, they had essentially defeated the Boer armies in the field before the end of the year, captured both enemy capitals and annexed the two republics to become part of the Empire. However, many of the Boer commandos remained in the field. Accurate, simple to maintain and needing only a supply of cartridges, the Mauser proved almost ideal for the hit-and-run guerrilla actions that characterized this phase of the war. Ultimately, however, the commandos found the mobility they depended on was eroded by the construction of chains of blockhouses and barbed wire, while their ability to live off the land was reduced by a British 'scorched earth' policy that burned farmhouses and crops, poisoned water sources and swept non-combatants off to detention camps. By the time the last of the 'bitter enders' finally gave up their struggle in 1902, the majority had long abandoned their Mausers for rifles taken from British casualties, as the only source of fresh ammunition was from captured stocks.

WORLD WAR I

The Mauser in the wider battle

The Gew 98 had seen limited combat with the German expeditionary force despatched to China during the Boxer Rebellion, and during the brutal punitive campaign against the rebellious Herero tribe in German South West Africa, but World War I provided its first real test. France had long desired revenge for its defeat in the Franco-Prussian War, and its military alliances with Britain and (more importantly) Russia threatened Germany and its Austro-Hungarian ally with encirclement in any future war. When the assassination of the Austro-Hungarian heir, Archduke Franz Ferdinand, in Sarajevo in July 1914 set the Austro-Hungarian Empire on a path to war with Russia's protégé, Serbia, it was only a matter of time until the various powers were dragged into a general conflict by their networks of alliances. The German war plan relied heavily on its ability to mobilize rapidly, knock France out of the war quickly and then transfer forces east across the efficient German rail network to oppose the Russians before the latter had completed their own more sluggish mobilization.

Ironically, the plan foundered on exactly the lesson the German Mauser had taught the British and Americans so expensively a decade earlier – that modern rifles tipped the tactical balance heavily in favour of the defender. Despite initial (if costly) success pushing the British and French forces back, the German advance was halted at the battle of the Marne (5–12 September 1914), where the Germans found it impossible to advance in the face of rapid, effective rifle fire from weapons equivalent to their own. Both sides dug themselves into an increasingly complex and sophisticated system of trenches that ultimately ran from the Swiss border to the sea. Germany now found itself fighting exactly the two-front war against France and Russia that it had wished to avoid, with the added complication of Britain having been drawn in on the French side by the German violation of Belgian neutrality. Most commanders expected the entrenchment to be a short phase before the return to 'normal' open warfare, based on relatively dense rifle firing lines suppressing the enemy before delivering a decisive charge with the bayonet. However, two key advances in technology had meant that rifles like the Mauser lost their place as ruler of the battlefield.

This photograph of a German infantryman with Gew 98 probably dates from before 1916, since he is wearing a leather *Pickelhaube* with canvas cover rather than a steel helmet. Note the obsolete single-compartment ammunition pouches, issued to make up manufacturing shortfalls, and the pocket lamp attached to a tunic buttonhole. (Tom Laemlein/ Armor Plate Press)

The first advance related to artillery. The adoption of the recoil cylinder, pioneered by the French M1897 75mm field gun, allowed much higher rates of fire without needing to re-lay the gun after each shot, while better battlefield communications allowed accurate indirect fire. These factors meant that packing forward trenches with riflemen inevitably meant taking extremely heavy casualties, and artillery fire forced commanders to disperse units into multiple deeper lines of positions. This dispersion hampered concentration of defensive fire, but artillery provided a solution to the problem it had itself created; defending troops could quickly bring down a devastating protective barrage on attackers, by field telephone or pre-arranged coloured flares.

The second advance related to machine guns. The German Army went to war in 1914 with six MG 08 machine guns per infantry regiment, roughly comparable to their opponents. However, while British regiments were essentially administrative organizations consisting of a variable number of battalions that might not be serving together – or even in the same theatre – each German regiment was a tactical unit containing three battalions, each with four rifle companies, plus a separate 13th machine-gun company. This meant that the German machine guns were centralized under the direct control of the regimental commander, and led to better utilization than the British and French approach of giving a pair to each battalion. Aside from their obvious ability to add significantly to the firepower of the depleted rifle firing lines, small numbers of machine guns were easier to protect than masses of infantry.

While the Allies regarded their trenches as jumping-off points for the next offensive, the Germans were on the strategic defensive for much of the war, and put considerable effort into constructing dugouts deep enough to survive anything short of a direct hit. Machine-gun teams sat out the heaviest preparatory bombardment in these, then raced up the steps to the trench parapet with their guns as soon as the shelling lifted, to put down a killing fire on the enemy infantry advancing behind the barrage. Machine guns quickly proved so indispensable that in German service their numbers were tripled by replacing the single regimental machine-gun company with a similar company in each of the regiment's three battalions, once enough guns became available in late 1916.

The standard German MG 08 was a water-cooled Maxim derivative. Although extremely reliable, it weighed nearly 70kg on its heavy sled mount with a full water jacket. It was an excellent defensive weapon, but difficult to move forward with the riflemen in the attack. Rather than develop a specialized light machine gun along the lines of the British Lewis or French Chauchat, the Germans opted to slim down an MG 08 to create the MG 08/15 light machine-gun version, though 'light' was a relative term; it still weighed 24kg loaded and with a full water jacket. Even so, the MG08/15 could be carried forward by attacking infantry, and by 1918 each infantry company had six, or two per platoon. With each gun served by a nine-man section (an NCO, a four-man gun team and four riflemen to provide close protection for the gun team), the machine gun, rather than the rifle, had clearly become the centre of the infantry platoon by the end of the war.

The M1918 T-Gewehr

When the first British tanks appeared in late 1916, the Germans found that although the vehicles were proof against rifle fire, they could be penetrated by the standard armour-piercing SmK bullet, originally intended for use against the loopholed armoured plates used by snipers. When the improved British Mark IV tank appeared in 1917, it had armour proof against even the SmK bullet.

The German response was to develop a massive 13.2×92mm cartridge, with a hardened steel-core bullet capable of penetrating even the improved armour. The round was to be used by both an anti-tank rifle, and by an enlarged version of the water cooled Maxim MG 08 machine gun, to be known as the MG 18. In the event, the MG 18 was too late to see service during the war, but the M1918 anti-tank rifle (also known as the *Tank-Gewehr*, or '[anti-] tank rifle') entered service in early 1918. It was a single-shot bolt-action design, based on a massively enlarged version of the Mauser action, and fitted with a pistol grip and bipod. The rifle weighed 18.5kg and was issued to two-man teams. A magazine-fed version was designed, but never entered production. The round it used could penetrate 25mm of armour at 250m. It was a solid round with no explosive element, however, and through it might ricochet around inside a vehicle to kill crew members, even tanks which suffered penetration were not always put out of action. In total, some 15,800 T-Gewehr weapons were produced. A few examples remained in service with the Reichswehr after World War I, but were replaced by new designs before World War II.

ABOVE The Mauser M1918 T-Gewehr and its 13.2×92mm cartridge. The three holes drilled in the cartridge and bolt are to deactivate the weapon, not original features. (Author's photograph, © Royal Armouries PR.1725)

New Zealand gunners with a captured T-Gewehr anti-tank rifle near Grévillers, August 1918. (© IWM Q 11264)

To put the relative importance of rifles into context, official German estimates in 1917 indicated that machine guns used between two-thirds and nine-tenths of the cartridges issued, and this ratio would only have increased, since the numbers of machine guns in service increased as the war dragged on, and the number of rifles did not. This did not mean that rifle fire was negligible in effect, as this German description of rifle fire against British troops advancing on the first day of the Somme indicates:

> … a murderous fire spewed against them from foxholes, shell-holes and what was left of the trenches. The gaunt and dust covered shapes of our soldiers, some of them in shirt sleeves, hastened out of their collapsing cellars and ploughed-up shelters. Seized by an indescribable lust for battle they stood, kneeled or lay flat as best enabled them to send a murderous massed fire into the continuous ranks of the British… Wave after wave was being cut down by the accurate fire which was being maintained by our officers, NCOs and men, regardless of hands which were bleeding from contact with the red-hot barrels of their rifles. (Quoted in Duffy 2006: 154)

The Mauser in the trenches

Faced with the need to mobilize far more men than planned, the Germans struggled to arm them at the start of the war. A total of 22,000 Mauser rifles produced under contract for China and Paraguay, but yet to be shipped, were seized and pressed into service, but this was a drop in the ocean. More importantly, large numbers of Gew 88 'Commission Rifles' were modified for the S-Munition and charger loading, either by the pre-war 88/05 conversion or the rather hastier wartime 88/14 conversion, and issued as a substitute rifle for front-line units. (The Gew 88 S was modified to use the S-Munition, but was still loaded via clips, rather than chargers.

A German soldier cleans his Gew 98 in a strikingly clean and dry section of trench; given the surviving trees, it is unlikely to be an active section of the line. (Tom Laemlein/Armor Plate Press)

Most were ultimately converted to charger loading via one of the other conversions.) Militia troops within Germany even found themselves equipped with old Gew 71 Mausers fitted with barrel liners for the 7.92mm round, as combat units received priority for more modern weapons. Even these additional weapons were not enough, and the Germans were forced to rely on captured rifles (mostly Russian Mosin-Nagants) to arm some of their replacement units.

One problem that quickly emerged was that the Gew 98 had been designed with open battle in mind. The changes to adapt it for the S-Munition meant the minimum distance the sights could be set for was 400m, much too far for close-quarters fighting, and an auxiliary *Hilfskorne* front sight was issued to give a minimum range of 100m. Meanwhile, the rifle itself was notably long and difficult to manoeuvre in the cramped quarters of

trenches and bunkers. The obvious solution was to issue more of the shorter, handier carbines. These rose from comprising 15 per cent of long arms issued in 1914 to 30 per cent by the end of the war, and became the weapon of choice for the *Sturmtrupp* assault units. Even so, the Mauser's slow rate of fire meant that trench raiders and troops expecting close fighting increasingly abandoned the rifle in favour of the hand grenade, pistols fitted with shoulder stocks and extended magazines to turn them into semi-automatic carbines, and melee weapons such as sharpened entrenching tools and trench clubs. The ultimate solution was the development of submachine guns such as the Bergmann MP 18, but this appeared too late in the war to make much difference. In fairness to the Mauser, other armies had similar problems; it was a reflection of the general state of weapons technology, rather than a design failing of a particular weapon.

Keeping weapons clean and functional in the trenches was difficult. Mud clogging the bolt and getting into the action was the most serious problem, as it would quickly jam the weapon. Also, the long bolt handle that projected out at a right-angle snagged on nearby items. A German infantryman described conditions in November 1915: 'The dugouts were completely filled with water and mud ... Shooting was out of the question, for our rifles were completely covered with mud so that we could not open the bolt any more. It was the same with every man on guard' (quoted in Ulrich & Ziemann 2010: 136). To counter the ever-present mud, soldiers were issued fabric carbine protectors, or tied rags around the breech of their rifles, but cloth itself became saturated with mud, and the fabric had to be removed before the weapon could be fired. As a better alternative, the German Army developed several patterns of sheet-metal breech covers in the later years of the war, though they were never

A Gew 98 fitted with a sheet-metal bolt protector and 20-round extension magazine. (Author's photograph, © Royal Armouries PR.6414)

universally fitted, even to all newly produced rifles. The first pattern simply clipped over the bolt of the weapon, and prevented the weapon being used, but later versions attached permanently to the rifle and moved with the bolt, so the weapon could be fired with them in place.

One disadvantage of these breech covers was that they slowed down reloading, and an extended 'trench magazine' was developed to deal with this problem, though some magazines also were fitted to standard rifles without the breech protectors. These magazines replaced the floor plate of the standard internal magazine, and held 20 rounds (i.e. for a total of 25 rounds, including the five rounds in the standard magazine). They were permanently fixed to the gun, and were intended for reloading *in situ* with five of the standard chargers, rather than acting as a modern detachable box magazine. As a result, they did not actually increase rate of fire, and the strong magazine spring made it hard to push in the last charger of cartridges. They never become a standard fitting, and were dropped after the war.

Poison gas was another problem for the rifle, since it corroded and tarnished the metal, causing the rifle to jam. Ernest Jünger describes how 'the men were all busy greasing their rifles in accordance with the nostrums of "What To Do in a Gas Attack", because their barrels had been completely blackened by chlorine' (Jünger 2003: 81).

THE INTER-WAR PERIOD

With the Armistice in November 1918, most German soldiers marched back to their homeland in formed units, still under arms. This apparent discipline was more because it was the fastest and most efficient way to get home than from any desire to continue as soldiers, however, and the returning men quickly melted away once they reached their home garrisons, many taking their weapons with them. Nobody knows how many rifles disappeared into the swelling arsenals of the various local defence militias and *Freikorps* (paramilitary units of ex-soldiers, often used to put down communist unrest) that arose in the troubled years immediately after the war; the best guesses are at least 200,000–300,000 weapons, more than the 102,000 rifles and carbines the reformed Reichswehr were allowed under the Versailles Treaty. Other organizations,

including the Police, Forestry Service, Customs Officers and Prison Warders, were allowed to keep a further 63,227 rifles. These figures were a drop in the ocean compared to the six million rifles of various types collected for destruction by the Inter-Allied Military Control Commission, along with vast amounts of other military equipment. Most were destroyed by being stacked crosswise in outdoor piles 5m long, each containing around 500 rifles, then set on fire so that the wooden furniture burned and barrels and sights distorted in the heat.

While the two decades between the world wars proved to be a lean time for the Mauser in Germany, they saw a good deal of use elsewhere. The new Polish state had inherited the Danzig rifle factory as part of its war reparations from Germany, and lost no time in putting its products to use defending Poland's eastern frontier against the revolutionary Soviet armies. China's feuding warlords remained good customers, with some of them setting up factories to produce local copies of Mauser designs, to varying standards of quality. In South America, the armies of Bolivia and Paraguay were both armed with Mausers during the vicious war they fought over the inhospitable but supposedly oil-rich Chaco region (1932–35).

Mauser fought Mauser again in the Spanish Civil War (1936–39). The Republican government initially controlled most of the major arsenals, though as George Orwell describes, some of the weapons they contained were in poor condition:

> I got a shock of dismay when I saw the thing they gave me. It was a German Mauser dated 1896 – more than forty years old! It was rusty, the bolt was stiff, the wooden barrel-guard was split; one glance down the muzzle showed that it was corroded and past praying for. Most of the rifles were equally bad, some of them even worse. (Orwell 1989: 17)

The forces of the Nationalist rebels were built around a core of Spanish Army units, who retained their original issue Mauser rifles when their officers led the coup against the Republic. Although France and Britain remained neutral and persuaded the League of Nations to adopt a policy of 'non-intervention', both sides quickly acquired international sponsors. Nazi Germany dispatched the Condor Legion to support the Nationalists, exploiting the war as a testing ground for *Blitzkrieg* tactics, as well as sending significant aid, including large numbers of Mauser rifles. Meanwhile, the Republicans received help from the foreign volunteers of the International Brigades, and from the Soviet Union. Ironically, the Soviet aid included tens of thousands of Czech-made Mausers, purchased to provide weapons for the Republic without obviously breaching the Franco-British embargo.

WORLD WAR II

The Weimar Republic that governed Germany after World War I struggled to gain popular acceptance in its first years, because of the harsh reparations imposed after the war, post-war hyperinflation and political agitation and violence by extremists of left and right. Things began to improve in the mid-1920s, but the stock market crash of 1929 and the ensuing Great Depression of the 1930s caused mass unemployment, and the government lost its majority in the parliament, allowing the Nazi Party to gain power in 1933. Once in office, the Nazis quickly consolidated their hold on power, repudiated the limits placed on Germany's armed forces by the Versailles Treaty, and began an ambitious programme of re-armament and public works. These measures were followed by a series of opportunistic 'land grabs', including portions of Czechoslovakia and a union (*Anschluss*) with Austria. While Britain and France acquiesced to these at first, they eventually realized there would be no end to Hitler's demands. Ultimately, both declared war when Germany invaded Poland in 1939, though this was of little immediate help to the Poles, who were quickly overrun.

Despite German propaganda, the Panzer divisions never formed a majority of their forces, and some elements were equipped with rather less-advanced equipment. These men are Cossacks in German service, and seem unconcerned about the difficulties of using their Kar 98k rifles one-handed. (Cody Images)

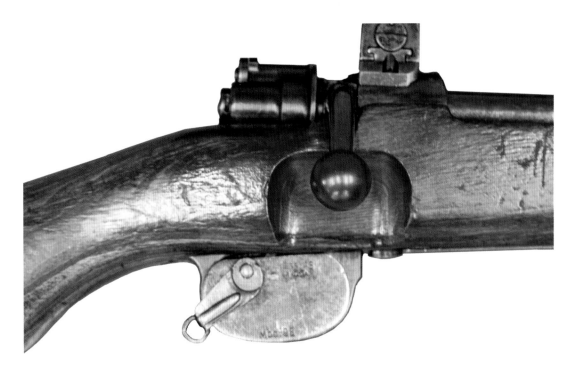

Despite the emphasis German propaganda placed on the tanks of the Panzer divisions, they were actually little more than an armoured cutting edge for a force still mostly composed of marching infantry, particularly during the early *Blitzkrieg* campaigns in Poland and Western Europe. When the German Army began to rearm and expand in the 1930s, it had learned the lessons of World War I. Each rifle squad was built around the excellent MG 34 or – from 1942 – MG 42 machine gun. Rather than using water cooling to prevent the barrels overheating during heavy fighting, these new machine guns used replaceable barrels – when the first barrel began to overheat, the crew simply swapped it out and put it aside to cool while they continued firing with the spare. The guns were thus much lighter, and easier to carry forward in the attack. The standard infantry squad now consisted of an NCO with an MP 38 or MP 40 submachine gun, a three-man machine-gun crew, and 4–6 riflemen. The machine gun provided most of the squad's firepower, while the riflemen acted as ammunition-carriers and provided local security for the machine-gun team.

Despite this, the Kar 98k still saw extensive combat use, particularly on the Eastern Front where partisan activities behind German lines meant that even rear-echelon troops had to be able to defend themselves if necessary. Partisans were not the only problem on the Eastern Front. German troops found that even the oil used to lubricate the moving parts of their weapons froze in the Russian winters. They quickly learned to follow the Soviets in using sunflower oil, which froze at lower temperatures, or (in extreme conditions) using a solvent such as petrol to remove all trace of lubricant and re-assemble the weapon 'dry'. Since fingers in thick winter gloves would not fit inside the trigger guard, oversize 'winter triggers' were also developed.

Although a solid and dependable weapon, the Kar 98k was increasingly coming up against US and Soviet semi-automatic rifles, and the Germans

The cold of the Eastern Front prompted the development of this winter trigger for the Kar 98k, since heavy winter gloves were too bulky to fit inside the trigger guard. Only a minority of rifles were fitted with such triggers, even in the East. (Author's photograph, © Royal Armouries PR.6446)

tried to replace it with more advanced weapons. Despite this effort, the desperate need for more weapons to replace losses kept the Kar 98k in full production until the end of the war, with various changes to speed up and simplify manufacture. Even then, production could not keep up with demand – when the Nazis finally organized their Volkssturm militia as a 'last-ditch' home guard in October 1944, it had to be armed with a mixture of captured rifles and carbines.

AFTER 1945

World War II left millions of Kar 98ks in the hands of the victorious Allies and their satellite states, but this time, there was no programme of mass destruction of weapons like that following World War I. Instead, these weapons quickly found users in the hands of new countries trying to make a place for themselves in the post-war world, or existing ones trying to hold on to what they already had. France pressed Kar 98k rifles into service in the immediate post-war period, including both captured weapons and new production rifles from factories in the French-occupied zone of Germany. Some saw service in Indochina, alongside Vichy-era French designs and US weapons provided as military aid.

The Soviet Union captured millions of Mauser rifles, and huge numbers were reconditioned (usually with a thick, dull re-bluing, and little attention to matching the serial numbers of parts) and stored against future need. Over the years, some of these 'Russian Capture' Mausers were supplied as military aid to various communist and revolutionary organizations, including the Viet Minh, People's Army of North Vietnam and the Viet Cong during the Indochina and Vietnam wars (1946–75). Other Soviet satellites often had similar programmes. Refurbished Mausers saw service with the East German Border Guards and Worker's Militia until replaced by more modern weapons. In Yugoslavia, the Zastava company refurbished tens of thousands, as well as producing a near-copy known as the M48. Thousands of these weapons reappeared during the Balkan wars of the 1990s.

Many former occupied nations received Mauser rifles to equip their re-established armed forces after the war. Norway provides a typical case; although the Kar 98k rifles initially issued were soon replaced in front-line service by American M1 Garand rifles received as military aid, the Mausers remained in second-line service, converted to fire the Garand's .30-06 cartridge. Some were even converted again to 7.62mm NATO, when Norway adopted a variant of the Heckler & Koch G3, and remained in service with some Home Guard units into the 1970s.

Another notable user was the new State of Israel. Established as a Jewish homeland by the United Nations when the British mandate in Palestine ended in May 1948, it was immediately attacked by a coalition of neighbouring Arab countries. The Israelis had anticipated this response, and prepared for it by purchasing weapons, including large numbers of Kar 98k rifles, despite an attempted arms embargo by the British. More Kar 98ks were purchased after the 1948 war, mostly from Czechoslovakia and FN of Belgium, and it became the standard Israeli rifle. Israel even purchased a production line to manufacture the Kar 98k themselves, but relatively few were produced before the Mauser was replaced by the more advanced FN FAL self-loader in the late 1950s. Many Israeli Mausers were converted to 7.62×51mm NATO to use the same ammunition as the FAL, and remained in use by support units through the 1967 and 1973 Arab-Israeli wars, before the last were sold or passed on as military aid.

Spain continued to use the Mauser-copy M43 until the adoption of the CETME automatic rifle in 1957, but few saw combat. Some Kar 98k rifles were briefly used by the West German border guards into the 1950s, but the last Mauser rifles in German military service are the wartime Kar 98k rifles used by the Bundeswehr's ceremonial *Wachbataillon* as drill weapons; all Nazi-era markings were removed from these weapons in 1995.

A storeroom at Solar aerodrome, Stavanger, holding some of the 30,000 Mauser rifles taken from the German forces in Norway after their surrender. (© IWM BU 9763)

MAUSER ACCESSORIES

Bayonets

The Gew 98 was accompanied by a new bayonet, the Seitengewehr (literally 'Sidearm') 98. With an overall length of 65cm, it featured a notably long – 53cm – blade, to match France's long Lebel rifle and its épée-like bayonet. In practice, the long and relatively thin Mauser blade proved fragile and prone to bending. It was superseded by the short-lived Seitengewehr 98/02, with a shorter and sturdier 44cm blade, and then the Seitengewehr 98/05, with a still-substantial 37cm blade. The hilts of all the Seitengewehr 98 bayonets featured quillons that curved back towards the hilt. These were much less effective at catching an opposing blade than the forward-swept quillons used by some other nations. All Mauser bayonets attached via a T-shaped bar fitted under the barrel. Though many bayonets of the time used a muzzle ring, Mauser avoided one since these altered the vibration harmonics of the barrel when fired, and thus affected accuracy.

Pioniere and some infantrymen were issued Seitengewehr 98 bayonets with saw teeth on the back edge of the blade. Although this variant was intended simply as a tool, Allied propaganda seized on its fearsome appearance. Many German troops became reluctant to carry these bayonets, fearing ill-treatment if captured carrying them. As a result, production of the sawback version ended in 1917, and most existing examples were relegated to rear-area troops or had their sawbacks ground off. Machine-gunners and other specialist troops were issued a smaller, more knife-like bayonet with a 26cm blade, a serrated back edge and a characteristic 'eagle head' pommel (the kurzes Seitengewehr 98, or 'Short Sidearm 98').

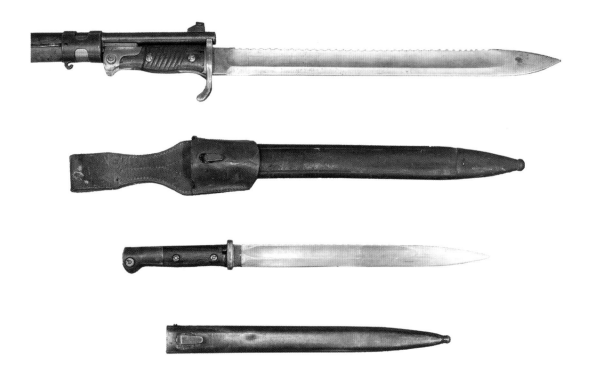

These remained the standard German bayonets throughout World War I, though shortages led to a flood of *Ersatz* ('substitute') designs, often of poor quality and some converted from obsolete or captured models. The most important of these was the Seitengewehr 84/98, commonly issued to men armed with carbines. It had a smaller (250mm) blade without quillons, and used less material as well as being lighter and handier in the trenches. When re-armament began in the 1930s, the Seitengewehr 84/98 was chosen as the new standard bayonet, and served throughout World War II with only minor modifications. The Wehrmacht put more faith in automatic weapons and grenades than in bayonets for close fighting, however, and the bayonet attachment finally disappeared from the *Kriegsmodell* versions of the Kar 98k to simplify production.

Scabbards were originally of leather, but these proved flimsy and were replaced by stronger and cheaper steel scabbards during World War I. *Troddeln* or bayonet knots in the company colour were attached to the bayonet frog, and were worn even in the field. Recruits bayoneted sandbags during training to build fighting spirit, and practised fighting with padded 'bayonets' mounted on dummy rifles. An anonymous deserter felt this training had done little to prepare him for actual bayonet fighting, however:

We fought like wild animals. For minutes there was bayonet fighting of a ferocity that defies description. We stabbed and hit like madmen – through the chest, the abdomen, no matter where. There was no semblance of regular bayonet fighting: that, by the way, can only be practised in the barracks yard. The butt-ends of our rifles swished through the air. Every skull that came in our way was smashed in … We forgot all around us and fought bloodthirstily without any calculation. (Anonymous 2013: 79)

Rifle grenades and grenade launchers

Trench warfare led to the rapid appearance of the first mass-produced hand grenades, and armies quickly began looking for a means of projecting such weapons further than they could be thrown. The Germans began the war with limited stocks of the experimental M13 rifle grenade – essentially an explosive-filled cylinder of cast iron, grooved to fragment and attached to a rod that fitted down the barrel of any Gew 98 rifle. A special blank cartridge launched the grenade out to a theoretical range of 320m, but accuracy was rather poor and the fuse assembly was not well thought out, being prone to both premature detonation and duds. The improved M14 was both safer and more reliable. Fitting metal stabilizer discs to both grenades improved accuracy very significantly, at the cost of reducing the range to 200m, though accuracy beyond that range without a disc was very poor anyway. Even so, the rods of the grenades tended to damage the rifle barrels. Recoil was very significant, and launching these grenades from the shoulder was not recommended. The rifle could be fired from a kneeling position with the butt on the ground, but increasingly, special launching racks, made from wood and fitted with dedicated sights, were used.

Meanwhile, the French introduced the ground-breaking Vivien-Bessière grenade launcher in 1916. The Germans promptly adopted a similar weapon, the Gewehrgranate 17 or *Schießbecher* ('Shooting Cup'), which completely replaced the earlier rodded rifle grenades. It consisted of a relatively large-diameter smoothbore cup that attached to the muzzle of the rifle. A short, cylindrical grenade slipped into the cup, and was fired by a normal live round. The bullet passed through a narrow channel through the centre of the grenade, throwing it in an arcing trajectory out to 150m, where it was detonated by a five-second time fuse. Although shorter-ranged and less powerful than the rodded rifle grenades, the M17 was much safer to use, and there was no need for special cartridges. Four discharger cups were issued per rifle company in 1917, doubling to eight per company during 1918.

In World War II, the Germans issued two grenade launchers. The first was the Gewehrgranatengerät zur Panzerbekampfung 40 ('Rifle Grenade Apparatus for

At top, a World War I M17 'Shooting Cup' on a Gew 98; at bottom, a Gewehrgranatengerät 42 on a Kar 98k, with its elaborate sheet-metal sight mounted on the left of the rifle. (Author's photograph, © Royal Armouries PR.12999 & PR.13004)

The round had to be carefully engaged with the rifling when loading the Gewehrgranatengerät launcher. (Tom Laemlein/Armor Plate Press)

Anti-tank Use'), which consisted of a tube that attached to the bayonet lug. An anti-tank grenade then slid over this barrel extension, and could be launched out to a maximum range of 100m. Relatively few were issued, mostly to airborne troops. It was replaced in 1942 by another cup-type grenade launcher, formally designated the Gewehrgranatengerät 42 but – unsurprisingly – also nicknamed the *Schießbecher*. This replaced all previous models, and was issued relatively widely, with 1.5 million launchers being produced before the end of the war; one was issued to each infantry and engineer squad. It had a much smaller bore (3cm) than the World War I-era M17, and unusually for a grenade launcher, it was rifled for better accuracy. This was especially useful, since recoil was low enough for it to be fired from the shoulder, like a normal rifle. It was therefore a viable weapon against armoured vehicles, which were very difficult to hit with indirect 'lob' shots. The launcher clamped over the end of the rifle barrel, and was aimed by a rather complicated sheet-metal sight (complete with a bubble level) that attached to the left side of the rifle. The sight was calibrated to 250m in 25m increments, although it was possible to get the high-explosive grenades to reach a little further. Against armoured vehicles, however, the effective range was around 100m against a stationery target, and 75m for a moving one. The weapon was issued with high-explosive rounds for use against infantry and field fortifications, and an anti-tank round for use against armoured vehicles. However, the initial anti-tank grenade had rather limited armour penetration, and a new anti-tank grenade with a larger-diameter head that protruded from the muzzle of the launcher was issued to supplement it.

The large anti-tank grenade had roughly twice the penetration of the earlier design, and was capable of penetrating 80mm of armour at an impact angle of 60 degrees; this halved to 40mm as the impact angle increased to 30 degrees. The grenade was theoretically powerful enough to penetrate the frontal armour of a Sherman or T-34, the most common Allied tanks, though it was not accurate enough to target the vulnerable points of a tank specifically. The high-explosive grenade could also be used as a hand grenade (roughly equivalent to the standard German 'egg grenade') by unscrewing the nose cap and pulling the igniter cord beneath. Neither of the anti-tank grenades could be used as hand grenades. Other rounds included inert training rounds and a special grenade for launching propaganda leaflets.

The World War II-era Gewehrgranatengerät reverted to the older method of using a blank cartridge to launch the grenade, rather than the live round employed by the M17. Each grenade was supplied with the correct blank cartridge attached to the tail by a paper band. Although this was less convenient than using a live round, and created the risk of firing a live round rather than a blank when a grenade was in place, it was felt worthwhile since it improved accuracy and permitted a more compact design.

In theory, the grenade-launching cup was carried in a belt pouch, and only mounted on the rifle when it was to be used to launch grenades. Normal rounds could be fired with the empty launcher in place, but it affected the point of aim of the rifle while it was attached. In practice, grenade launchers were often mounted semi-permanently and only removed when the unit was out of the front lines.

Silencers

During the 1930s and 1940s, the Wehrmacht and Waffen-SS developed several patterns of sound suppressors (*Schalldämpfer*), which significantly reduced the sound of a rifle shot. All used a number of baffles inside a cylindrical body to deflect and slow the sound waves, but were only really effective when used with the special sub-sonic *Nahpatrone* ('Close-Range Cartridge') ammunition. This ammunition significantly reduced the muzzle velocity (and thus the effective range) of the bullet; without it, there would still be the distinctive *crack* as the bullet broke the sound barrier. The combination of silencer and special ammunition apparently reduced the noise of a shot by about 75 per cent, but also reduced effective range from 600m+ to less than 300m. None was issued in large numbers. Most went to snipers, so they could fire without giving away their position. However, many disliked using them, since the reduced range often compromised the sniper's safety. As the silencers resemble the cylindrical grenade-launcher attachment, the two are commonly confused in photographs.

MAUSER VARIANTS

Paratrooper models

The Germans were among the first to realize the tactical possibilities of airborne troops, and their *Fallschirmjäger* achieved some notable successes during the *Blitzkrieg* operations early in World War II. Yet the standard German RZ 1 parachute issued to airborne troops, and its successor the RZ 16, were both inferior to Allied parachutes, since the German parachutes' canopy lines didn't meet to form a pair of risers linked to each shoulder, but converged to a single attachment point between the shoulder blades. This configuration meant that the parachutes were much less controllable, and usually resulted in the jumper landing relatively hard and on his front, increasing jump injuries and making it much more

These *Fallschirmjäger* have managed to retrieve their Kar 98k rifles from weapons containers during a training exercise. It wouldn't always prove so easy in real combat. (Cody Images)

The hinge of the folding stock of the prototype paratrooper version of the Kar 98k. (Author's photograph, © Royal Armouries PR.6441)

A standard Gew 33/40 (top) showing the odd protective plate on the butt, and the prototype folding-stock version (bottom). The Gew 33/40 was the standard weapon for German mountain troops. (Author's photograph, © Royal Armouries PR.6309 & PR.6307)

difficult to carry weapons during a drop. As a result, while Allied parachutists carried their normal personal weapons during the drop, German parachutists jumped with only a pistol, and their weapons were dropped in separate containers. It was not the ideal system; during the battle of Crete in 1941, many *Fallschirmjäger* were pinned down on their landing zones by unexpectedly strong Allied resistance and were unable to reach their weapons containers to fight back effectively. It was possible to jump with an MP 40 submachine gun tucked under the parachute harness or strapped to a thigh, but the limited number available and their short effective range meant that only one airborne soldier in four carried one of these weapons.

In an attempt to produce a rifle that could be carried during a parachute jump, the Germans developed folding-stock versions of both the Kar 98k and Gew 33/40 rifles; a hinge just behind the trigger allowed the wooden butt to fold forward. Although the folding butt reduced the weapons' length significantly, it was still too long, and a 'take-down' version of the Kar 98k was produced. This rifle split into two sections

using an interrupted thread just ahead of the chamber, so the rifle could be carried as two halves. In the event, the heavy casualties suffered during the Crete operation convinced Hitler that large-scale airborne operations were too costly, and the *Fallschirmjäger* were effectively used as elite infantry for the rest of the war. As a result, none of the special paratrooper versions of the Kar 98k progressed beyond the prototype stage.

Mauser sniper rifles. From the top: a Kar 98k with the 1.5× Zf 41 scope; Kar 98k with 4× scope on side-rail mount; Kar 98k with 4× Zf 39 scope on turret mount; World War I-era Gew 98 with Goerz scope. (Author's photograph, © Royal Armouries PR.6444, PR.6445, PR.6446 & PR.6424)

Sniper models in World War I

Like the other powers, Germany began World War I without any organized sniping programme. However, the nation had the advantage that hunting and shooting using telescopic-sighted rifles had been more common in civilian life before the war than in France or Britain, where hunting was much more limited and the most common sporting weapon was the shotgun. Also, production of the high-quality optical glass used in telescopic sights was a German speciality.

Once trench warfare became established, the Germans were quickly able to requisition or purchase some numbers of commercial telescopic-sighted rifles. Only rifles with Mauser actions and in 7.92mm calibre were taken, but many were chambered for the older round-nosed Patrone 88, rather than the current military pattern. To prevent accidents, these were fitted with an engraved metal plaque with a picture of the round-nosed Patrone 88 and the warning *Nur für Patrone-88, keine S-Munition verwenden* ('Only for 88-Cartridge, do not use S-ammunition').

57

These weapons were swiftly followed into service by the Scharfschützengewehr 98, a purpose-built sniping rifle capable of using standard military ammunition. They were based on Gew 98 rifles selected for accuracy and fitted with a variety of commercial telescopic sights, usually of 3–4× magnification. (A 3× sight means that a target 600m away will appear the same size in the sight as a target 200m away seen with the naked eye.) It was relatively easy to fit scopes to the basic Mauser design, with its solid bridges ahead and behind the bolt, and a variety of commercial mounting systems were used. The only other modification required was to bend the straight bolt handle downwards, to avoid fouling on the scope. An estimated 20,000 were produced and issued to marksmen, who were generally exempted from other duties to concentrate on sniping.

The Prussian authorities generally preferred rifles with sights offset to the left to facilitate charger loading, while Bavaria preferred telescopic sights mounted directly above the bore; although this made quick reloading with chargers difficult, it allowed a much more natural aiming position. It also made using loopholed armour plates to protect the sniper much more practical, since the aperture could be narrower than for a rifle with an offset scope.

The availability of sniping rifles and a pool of men with civilian experience as hunters or foresters gave the Germans a significant advantage in the sniping field for the first two years of the war. It was not until 1916 that the British really caught up, and indeed went on to take the advantage themselves by introducing a structured programme to produce well-trained snipers in quantity. Meanwhile, the Germans found that their pool of men with pre-war experience was dwindling, and although ad hoc sniping schools were set up to train replacements, they varied in quality, and could not train enough men to meet the demand. One sniper lamented that the only instruction he had received was an hour to read the manual that accompanied his telescopic sight. The Germans did surprisingly little to preserve the snipers they did have; although the three sniping rifles issued to each rifle company were supposed to be withdrawn before an attack, to prevent them being lost or damaged, no similar measures were taken to preserve the trained men who used them. Instead, they went forward alongside their comrades, carrying standard rifles. By the second half of the war, British snipers increasingly dominated their German adversaries, though the latter maintained their advantage over both the French and Russians, neither of whom really developed a sniping infrastructure of their own.

Sniper models in World War II

The post-war Reichswehr had little interest in sniping, believing it was purely a product of trench warfare, which it did not expect to recur. Indeed, it actually began to sell off the wartime sniping rifles still held in stock in the 1930s. Although this sell-off ended with the rearmament pursued after the Nazis came to power, Germany's new rulers saw no place for such weapons in the *Blitzkrieg* style of armoured warfare now

A German sniper. The small size and long eye relief of the 1.5× Zf 41 telescopic sight is very apparent in this view. It essentially attached to the rear-sight base, rather than mounting over the receiver as in the case of the larger-magnification sights. This photo is almost certainly a posed shot; although the man to the shooter's right is using an observation periscope, his two comrades exposing their heads rather defeats the point. (Tom Laemlein/Armor Plate Press)

envisaged. The Wehrmacht thus began World War II with no trained snipers, no sniper training programme and few sniper rifles. Experience in the Polish campaign led to the recommendation that one soldier in each rifle squad should have a telescopic sight for long-range shooting. The result was the Zf 41, (*Zielfernrohr*, or 'Telescopic Sight') a very small 1.5× magnification sight. It had an extremely long eye relief, mounting on the existing rear-sight base, which meant it did not interfere with charger loading. Although the small size made it relatively convenient, the low magnification meant that it was more of a weapon for a squad-level 'dedicated marksman' than a proper sniper's tool, though in fairness, that was exactly the role for which it was intended.

With the invasion of the Soviet Union in 1941, however, the Wehrmacht found itself facing the Red Army. The latter had wholeheartedly embraced sniping in the 1930s, and the Germans found themselves at a significant disadvantage in both equipment and training. Many German snipers used captured Russian sniper rifles, until equivalent German weapons appeared. These used a variety of scopes and mounts, all of 4× magnification and classified under the general designation of Zf 39 and attached to Kar 98k weapons selected for accuracy. Most were mounted directly over the bore, and the rifle therefore had to be loaded with individual rounds rather than chargers. Some higher-magnification scopes were used, but since field of view decreases as magnification rises, sights of more than 6× power were rarely practical. A few Kar 98k weapons were fitted with the 4× Zf 4 sight designed for the Gew 43, but this was unusual.

Despite strenuous efforts, supply of these telescopic sights never came close to meeting demand, and a bewildering variety of types saw service to make up the numbers. The low-powered Zf 41 remained by far the commonest scope in the German inventory, accounting for more than half the 200,000 telescopic-sighted rifles produced. It had originally been intended that the semi-automatic Gew 43 would be used by snipers, but they proved less accurate than the older Kar 98k, and were mostly only used with the compact Zf 41 marksman's scope.

Since none of the Western Allies had such a system of both 'dedicated marksmen' and 'real snipers', it led to much confusion about the both the numbers of snipers the Germans deployed and their standard of training,

with some commentators condemning the poor quality of German snipers, without realizing that what they had encountered were simply section-level marksmen. Training men as snipers was as important for the Germans as producing weapons for them to use, but courses needed instructors, who themselves had to learn their craft in the harsh school of experience, and it was 1943 before the Wehrmacht sniping schools were training significant numbers of snipers. Even then, the schools were never able to cope with demand, and some men became successful snipers without receiving formal tuition, often using captured Soviet rifles.

The course at a typical sniping school was four weeks long, and covered fieldcraft, personal camouflage and intelligence-gathering as well as marksmanship. The latter was covered extensively, both through conventional range work and using small-bore rifles on miniature terrain models complete with fields, villages and roads. As part of the course at the school, the new sniper was issued a rifle which remained with him when he returned to the front, to avoid weapons being damaged in transit or 'purloined' by rear-echelon units. Telescopic sights were not generally kept fitted to rifles when out of action, to avoid their being damaged or knocked out of alignment; they were issued with rigid leather or metal cases, usually with belt attachments.

A series of awards existed for successful snipers, with a surprisingly bureaucratic process to receive them. Only 'sniper kills' counted, not casualties inflicted defending a position during an attack, and such kills had to be confirmed by an officer or NCO. Initially, the award received was a silver stripe for every ten kills, but in late 1944 this was replaced by an oval badge in three grades, for 20, 40 and 60 kills respectively, though kills before the introduction of the new badge were not counted. Many men were reluctant to wear these badges, fearing brutal repercussions if captured while doing so. The German sniper Sepp Allerberger believed that no sane marksman would wear such a badge in battle, and posted his home as soon as he received it, while the British sniping instructor Charles Shore commented that he had never seen such a badge worn. Snipers on the Eastern Front could expect especially harsh treatment if captured, even without the kill badges; most carried pistols, grenades or submachine guns for last-ditch personal defence. Given the documented instances of captured German snipers being tortured before being killed, many felt it was better to die fighting,

Booty Mausers in Axis service

During the first *Blitzkrieg* campaigns, the German armed forces captured vast quantities of military equipment, much of which was recycled to arm second-line or occupation troops. Most of these weapons are outside the scope of this book, but some of the captured weapons were actually Mauser derivatives. Most obviously, when the Czech arms industry fell into German hands in 1938, this included the manufacturing plants for both the vz. 24 rifle and vz. 33 carbine ('vz' indicates *vzor*, or 'model').

The vz. 24 was a shortened Gew 98 derivative, built on a production line sold to the Czechs after World War I. It was almost identical to the Kar 98k, with the main differences being the Czech weapon's straight bolt handle, different sights and sling attachments and a solid walnut stock. Existing stocks of Czech rifles were taken directly into Wehrmacht service as the Gew 24(t) (German designations for captured weapons used a letter to indicate national origins, in this case 't' for *tschechoslowakisch*.) Meanwhile, production of the vz. 24 continued, with the products becoming more and more like the Kar 98k as stocks of Czech parts were used up. Many of the rifles produced went to Germany's ally Romania, but others were used by the German forces. The plant switched over to producing standard Kar 98k rifles in 1942.

The vz. 33 was a short carbine with a 490mm barrel. It was intended for *Gebirgsjäger* (mountain troops), and built on the same 'small ring' receiver as the original Kar 98AZ. Unusually, the left side of the butt was fitted with a sheet-metal plate, apparently to protect it from damage when used as an alpenstock – a short walking stick used when scrambling or mountaineering. Like the earlier short carbines, it suffered from significant recoil and muzzle flash. Captured examples were taken into German service as the Gew 33/40, while new examples (with minor modifications to the sling fittings, etc.) continued to be produced until 1942, when the Brno factory making it switched over to manufacturing the Kar 98k. It became the standard weapon of the *Gebirgsjäger*. Total production was just under 156,000, with the great majority (131,000) being produced under German occupation. A few prototypes with folding stocks were developed as possible airborne weapons, but never entered production.

After World War I, the former German territory given to the new Polish state as war reparations included the arms factory at Danzig, which produced Gew 98 rifles. The Poles used its machinery to produce weapons for their own forces during their war with the Soviet Union (1919–21). The rifles produced were initially almost identical to their World War I German predecessors, but in 1929, the Poles introduced a new design, the wz. 1929. Apart from sights, sling fittings and handguard, it was identical to the German Kar 98k. Thousands of these rifles, in various stages of completion when the Germans arrived, were finished as Gew 29/40 rifles, with the original Polish markings re-stamped into German ones. The production run was relatively short, and most of the 50,000 rifles appear to have gone to the Kriegsmarine and Luftwaffe before the Polish factories switched to producing standard Kar 98k rifles.

SS Mausers

While approving of Nazi rearmament policies during the 1930s, the Army high command was very concerned to maintain the Army's position as the primary armed force of the German state. This obviously brought it into conflict with the SA and later the SS, both arms of the Nazi Party with aspirations to become military forces in their own right. The Army actually pre-empted the entire production of the DRP Mauser to prevent them going to the SA, and Hitler ultimately purged the SA 'brownshirts' after gaining power, because of concerns over their loyalties and to keep the support of the Army.

While the SS was unquestionably loyal to the Nazi regime, Hitler's need to keep the Army's support meant that the SS were given very limited access to military weapons in the years immediately after the Nazis gained power. Even the elite honour guard of the SS, *Leibstandarte-SS Adolf Hitler*, had to parade with reworked Gew 98 rifles when the Italian leader Mussolini made a state visit in September 1937, rather than the new-production Kar 98k weapons carried by the Army and Luftwaffe honour guards at the same event. From 1940, the Waffen-SS (the combat arm of the SS) became the fourth official branch of the Wehrmacht, agreeing to come under Wehrmacht command in return for being equipped from the Wehrmacht supply chain. SS weapons obtained before this point carried commercial proof marks, rather than military ones, while those obtained afterwards had normal military proof marks.

An honour guard from the *Leibstandarte-SS Adolf Hitler* in Munich, 1935. The unit was expanded from a company to a motorized regiment after its part in the purge of Ernst Röhm's SA, and ultimately into a Panzer division. (Cody Images)

REPLACING THE MAUSER

Early Mauser self-loaders

While demonstrating his new C 96 self-loading pistol (the famous 'Mauser broomhandle') in 1896, Paul Mauser was asked by the Kaiser himself when a self-loading infantry rifle would be available. Perhaps a little too confidently, Mauser told him 'Perhaps in five years, Your Majesty.' In fact, though Mauser registered a number of patents over the next decade, it became clear that he had underestimated the difficulties. They were to cost him his left eye in 1901, when one of his experimental self-loaders exploded in his hands.

Paul Mauser's first designs were based on his proven self-loading pistol, with its recoiling barrel. However, this mechanism proved difficult to adapt to a full-power rifle cartridge, and Mauser ultimately abandoned this line of work as impractical. In 1908, he switched to a design using a fixed barrel and inertial locking. Although the design worked, it suffered from unreliable ejection, and only operated dependably with greased cartridges. This was clearly not practical for an infantry rifle, but a limited number were modified during World War I, for use by aircraft observers and airship crew. These modified carbines were fitted with a short vertical grip ahead of a detachable 25-round box magazine, which both increased firepower and limited the amount of dirt the greased cartridges picked up. Only a few thousand were produced in 1916–17, as the 'Mauser self-loading carbine'. Interest in self-loading rifles re-emerged with the start of rearmament in the 1930s. The Mauser design team reverted to the recoiling barrel and an integral ten-shot magazine for the Gew 35, a design produced in 1935 but which only reached small-scale troop trials.

Ironically, throughout this period, Mauser's engineers were very reluctant to use the gas system used in most modern self-loaders, since they were concerned that the barrel would be weakened by drilling a hole in it to tap off gas. This attitude was shared by much of the German armament establishment, and when the Army finally issued a requirement for a self-loading rifle in 1940, the key points of the specification included the following: the barrel was not to be bored to tap off gas; no part of the

A pair of early Mauser self-loaders – an unsuccessful 1898 flap-locking design (top) and one of the 1915 self-loaders before its transformation into the magazine-fed flyer's carbine. (Author's photograph, © Royal Armouries PR.6657 & PR.6658)

upper receiver was to move as part of the loading cycle; if the automatic mechanism failed, it must be possible to use the rifle manually in the same way as the existing 98 models. Mauser kept carefully to the criteria set out in the specification, producing the Gew 41(M). The mechanism used propellant gas tapped off via a cone-shaped gas-trap attachment at the muzzle to work the action. The weapon retained a ten-round integral magazine loaded from standard five-round chargers, and a manual bolt assembly as a backup. Only 20,000 were made, for troop trials.

Although Mauser had kept closely to the specification, the weapon's competitor – the Walther Gew 41(W) – had ignored several of the requirements. However, this gave the Walther team freedom to design a more practical self-loading rifle, which performed better in the trials and was put into production.

Semi-automatic and assault rifles

The Walther-designed Gew 41(W) was produced in relatively low numbers (around 120,000 rifles), but was actually heavier and less reliable than the basic Kar 98k and offered only a small increase in firepower, since its ten-round integral magazine was still loaded from the standard five-round chargers. By 1943, experience with captured examples of the Soviet Tokarev self-loading rifles had finally persuaded the Germans that boring the barrel to tap off gas was viable. The awkward gas-trap system of the Gew 41(W) was replaced by a conventional gas piston to create the Gew 43, which also featured a detachable ten-round box for faster reloading, and a number of simplifications to speed up production. The Gew 43 was intended to replace the Kar 98k, and over 400,000 were produced, but meanwhile, the Germans had been working on other, more radical designs.

The Luftwaffe had experimented with the FG 42 (*Fallschirmjägergewehr*, or 'Paratrooper Rifle') a selective-fire weapon intended to maximize firepower during airborne operations. It fired the standard 7.92×57mm cartridge from a 20-round box magazine, giving it almost the firepower of a light machine gun, but was roughly the size and weight of the standard rifle. However, the combination of a powerful round and a light weapon made it difficult to control when firing on full-automatic, and relatively few were made.

Like all rifle cartridges of its day, the 7.92×57mm cartridge had been designed for open warfare at relatively long ranges of up to 1,000m. However, research showed that there was little likelihood of the average infantryman actually hitting anything at that range under combat conditions, and that most firefights actually took place at ranges of 300m or less. The Germans therefore developed a shortened 7.92×33mm version of their standard rifle cartridge, known as the 7.92mm *kurz* ('short'). This was adequate for the shorter ranges at which most combat actually took place, was lighter for the soldier to carry, and used less strategic material to produce. Its smaller propellant load meant lower recoil than the full-sized round, allowing use in a selective-fire weapon.

The prototype MKb 42(H) (*Maschinenkarabiner*, or 'Machine Carbine') developed around the new round was a lightweight weapon that

made extensive use of cheap stamped (rather than machined) components and was capable of selective fire from a curved 30-round magazine – effectively it was the first modern 'assault rifle'. It was developed into the MP 43 and MP 44 assault rifles, which were intended to replace both the Kar 98k and the MP 40 submachine gun, with some 426,000 being produced. Yet the harsh reality was that German industry – increasingly short of skilled labour and raw materials, and under Allied bombing day and night – simply couldn't produce the new weapons in sufficient quantity. Despite their advantages, only a million or so of the various semi-automatic and assault rifles were produced, compared to 14 million of the simple and reliable Kar 98k, which remained in full production to the end of the war.

The Mauser company itself developed a new assault-rifle design (the so-called 'Gerät 06H') using roller locking, which would have been even cheaper to produce than the MP 44, but the war ended before it could be fully developed.

A selection of the weapons intended to replace the Kar 98k. From top: Mauser's Gew 41(M); two versions of the Walther Gew 43(W); and the late and early versions of the FG 42 selective-fire airborne rifle, with an MP 44 vertically on the right. (Author's photograph, © Royal Armouries PR.6665, PR.719, PR.6662, PR.1019, PR.6669 & XII.9114)

IMPACT
The right arm of the German soldier

IMPACT ON THE USER

The opinions which count most about a weapon are those of the men who actually carried and used it. Although some might complain of the weight of the Mauser rifle, or the cleaning required to keep it functional and rust-free in grim conditions, few questioned its accuracy or reliability. Indeed, the rifle was generally more accurate than the men who used it. One of the reasons the semi-automatic rifles never fully replaced the Kar 98k as sniper rifles was that despite the best efforts of their designers, the older rifle was still a more inherently accurate weapon. Ernst Jünger gives an example of what one could do in the hands of a good infantry shot, let alone a sniper:

> I spotted a British soldier breaking cover behind the third enemy line, the khaki uniform clearly visible against the sky. I grabbed the nearest sentry's rifle, set the sights to six hundred, aimed quickly, just in front of the man's head, and fired. He took another three steps, then collapsed on to his back, as though his legs had been taken away from him, flapped his arms once or twice, and rolled into a shell crater. (Jünger 2003: 126)

Most users found the Gew 98 over-long, but it was several years after its introduction before the British and US armies adopted the first so-called 'universal' rifles, short enough to replace both rifle and carbine. As it was, carbines made up an increasing percentage of Mausers issued, until the adoption of the Kar 98k solved the problem.

If the Mauser had a weak point, it was the relatively slow rate of fire. Gottlieb Biderman, serving on the Eastern Front with 132. Infanterie-Division, felt outgunned by his Russian opponents:

All were equipped with semiautomatic rifles or short-barreled submachine guns that were capable of firing seventy-two rounds from drum magazines. I took one of the submachine guns and several drum magazines from one of the prisoners for my own use, as I no longer placed much faith in the slow-firing 98k carbine for close combat. I felt more confident equipped with the high-capacity automatic weapon, and it was to remain with me for many months. (Biderman 2000: 53–54)

Others felt it was better to hit with one bullet than miss with several. William Lubbeck was given an MP 40 submachine gun to replace his rifle when he became a forward artillery observer with 58. Infanterie-Division, but was not impressed: 'Inaccurate beyond any distance greater than about 50 feet, the fire of the MP-40 resembled that of a shotgun more than a rifle. Though it was the standard weapon for a forward observer, I would have preferred to retain my Mauser' (Lubbeck 2006: 96).

Despite initial success in Operation *Barbarossa* in 1941, the Wehrmacht found itself unprepared for the ferocious Russian winter. Weapons iced up, gun oil froze, and men had to wear gloves even when using weapons, or risk losing fingers to frostbite. Note the man on the right, loading a fresh charger into his rifle. (Tom Laemlein/Armor Plate Press)

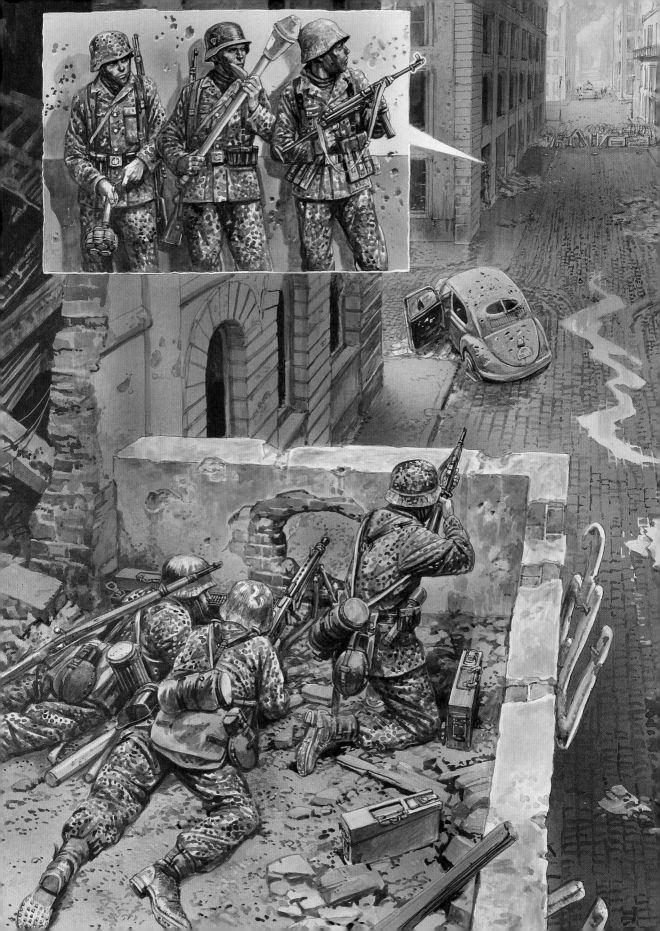

IMPACT ON THE BATTLEFIELD

When it was first introduced, the relatively quick-firing high-velocity bolt-action rifle utterly dominated the battlefield, and rendered the old tactical thinking obsolete, as experiences in the Spanish–American and 2nd Anglo-Boer wars showed. However, its dominance was short-lived, and its place was rapidly usurped by two new technical revolutions: much-improved artillery, and the machine gun. Statistics show that about 60 per cent of Allied casualties in both world wars were caused by mortars and artillery. Most of the remainder were caused by bullets, though given the proportion of rounds fired from machine guns as opposed to rifles, it is likely that the former inflicted between 50 per cent and 75 per cent of the bullet wounds recorded, leaving rifles inflicting only 10–20 per cent of the total casualties suffered by the enemy. Given the inherent accuracy of the Mauser design, why did it inflict such a low percentage of casualties?

The most obvious reason is that although even an indifferent rifle shot can rack up a good score on a firing range, shooting under combat conditions is a very different proposition. In his book *Firing Line*, Richard Holmes analyses an action in the Ypres Salient in 1914. While it involves British troops rather than German, it provides a useful measure of likely effectiveness. His figures suggest that the well-trained British regulars involved, firing under good conditions at targets mostly in the open, expended just under 27

The fall of Berlin, April 1945 (previous pages)

Although these Waffen-SS soldiers wear late-war *Erbsenmuster* camouflage uniforms, weapons like the MP 44 were never available in sufficient numbers, and the Kar 98k remained the most common German infantry weapon to the end of the war. This squad intends to use its full range of weapons to inflict the maximum casualties and delay on the advancing Soviets. Although the barricade across the street is not a significant obstacle, it shields the pair of anti-tank *Tellerminen* immediately behind, which would give any Soviet vehicle crashing through an unpleasant shock. The friction-igniter pull-cords of a pair of concealed stick grenades are tied into the barricade, complicating any attempt to remove it, even under cover of darkness; as well as the fragmentation effect, the noise of the grenade detonation would bring down pre-registered machine-gun fire on the troops attempting to remove the obstacle. The cornerstone of the defence is the squad's MG 42 machine gun, posted well back to take advantage of its range. The squad's sharpshooter has positioned himself opposite, back from the window to avoid being spotted. His small 1.5× Zf 41 scope offers low magnification for proper sniping, but is perfectly adequate in this urban environment, allowing him to enfilade any attackers taking cover from the machine gun. He will also pick off tank commanders exposing their heads, forcing them to 'close up' their hatches and lose vision, making them vulnerable to tank-killer teams. The section leader (with MP 40) and two men armed with *Panzerfäuste* and bundle charges wait to launch a surprise attack at close range on any Soviet tank that gets past the barricade, before falling back through the ruins under the covering rifle fire from the rest of the squad. Finally, a soldier with a grenade launcher fitted to his rifle has one of the large anti-tank grenades loaded; although inferior to the *Panzerfaust* as a tank killer, it did allow threats to be engaged at longer ranges than a hand-thrown grenade. One of his companions is careful to watch the squad's rear; enemy soldiers working their way around a position presented an ever-present danger in urban combat.

rounds for every casualty inflicted (Holmes 1994: 169). It is worth noting, however, that the sheer volume of fire the fast-shooting British put out compensated for the relatively low hit rate, and that they beat off the attackers. In other instances, rifle rounds were simply not aimed at all, as Ernst Jünger describes: 'Often you can hear the enemy working on his wire entanglements. Then you empty your magazine in his direction. Not only because those are the standing instructions, but also because you feel some pleasure as you do it. "Let them feel the pressure for a change. Who knows, perhaps you even managed to hit one of them"' (Jünger 2003: 45).

Any of the Mauser rifles would be capable of a sustained rate of 10–15 aimed shots per minute, in the hands of a trained soldier, though suitable targets would rarely present themselves continuously in real combat. The rifle did become hot with sustained firing; some soldiers talked of the barrels of their weapons becoming too hot to touch and even charring the wood of the forestock, but a soldier would have fired all the initial load of ammunition in his pouches before this point. Perhaps the best explanation why rifles like the Mauser accounted for such a low percentage of casualties is not that they were poor at inflicting

Kar 98k-equipped soldiers of the Deutsches Afrikakorps on parade in June 1941. The sun helmets were not popular, and were soon replaced by field caps. (Cody Images)

casualties, but that artillery and machine guns were superlatively good at doing so, as accounts from both world wars attest. It is also worth remembering that even rounds that miss have an effect, forcing the enemy to seek cover and constraining his actions, and that part of the role of the infantry rifle was to reduce enemy mobility, as well as to inflict casualties.

IMPACT ON THE ENEMY

It is ironic that the standard German 7.92×57mm rifle cartridge used through both world wars is generally known as the 7.92mm Mauser or, less frequently, as the 8mm Mauser. It was actually developed for the Gew 88 'Commission Rifle', and Paul Mauser had no involvement in its design. No matter who developed it, it was a highly efficient round. The standard round ('ball ammunition', in military parlance) evolved from the round-nosed Patrone 88, through the ballistically superior pointed S-Munition of 1905 to the heavier sS-Patrone, originally introduced purely for machine guns during World War I, but standard for rifles from the 1930s.

All of these were relatively heavy, high-velocity bullets; the S-Munition's 9.7g bullet left the muzzle at 878m/sec, giving a muzzle energy of 3,857J. (A joule is a standard unit of force, sufficient to raise a weight of 100g by 1m.) For comparison, a .45in ACP round from a Colt M1911 delivers around 500J, and a standard 5.56mm SS109 round from an M16A2 assault rifle delivers around 1,770J. This does not imply a round from a Kar 98k is twice as lethal as one from an M16, or seven times as lethal as being hit by a .45in; wound location is more important than sheer power, and different rounds do not behave identically when they strike a body. In many cases, excess energy is wasted as the bullet continues straight through the target in a so-called 'shoot through' without transferring all its energy. However, it does serve as a basis for comparison.

For those who prefer to envisage bullet effects in more concrete terms, the 1943 German infantry handbook indicates that the sS-Patrone will penetrate 900mm of sand or 850mm of dry pine wood at 400m, and 7mm iron or 3mm steel at 500m. It rather regretfully notes that a full-thickness brick wall will only be penetrated by a lucky single shot, but that sustained fire will quickly destroy such a wall (Reibart 2010: 286). The writer George Orwell describes, with classic British understatement, being hit by a Mauser bullet while serving with the anarchist POUM militia during the Spanish Civil War:

> The whole experience of being hit by a bullet is very interesting and I think it is worth describing in detail.... Roughly speaking it was the sensation of being at the centre of an explosion. There seemed to be a loud bang and a blinding flash of light all around me, and I felt a tremendous shock – no pain, only a violent shock, such as you get from an electric terminal; with it a sense of utter weakness, a feeling of being stricken and shrivelled up to nothing. The sandbags in front of me receded into immense distance. I fancy you would feel much the same if you were struck by lightning. (Orwell 1989: 143)

Orwell was very lucky he survived to describe his experience; being hit in the head or neck by a Mauser bullet (as he was) generally had fatal consequences. Wounds to the torso and abdomen might be survivable, if the casualty received surgical attention reasonably quickly. Without this, death from internal bleeding or subsequent infection was only too likely. When a high-velocity bullet struck one of the long bones of the limbs, it tended not just to break but to shatter it, reducing a significant length of the bone to jagged splinters. Aside from the removal of these splinters being time-consuming for the already overworked medical staff, the simple destruction of bone meant that even if amputation could be avoided, the man was likely to be left with a permanent limp. Even 'flesh wounds' that missed bones or major organs could be extremely serious. Aside from the obvious tearing of muscle, the bullet tended to carry fragments of uniform deep into the wound, where they could lead to infection unless carefully removed. This was a particular problem on World War I's Western Front, where the entire battlefield was heavily contaminated with decomposition bacteria from thousands of unburied corpses. Since modern antibiotics were not available until after World War II, there were few ways to treat the ensuing gangrene other than amputation, and even that was not always successful.

The pointed design of the *Spitzer* bullets, with the majority of mass towards the rear, meant that they tended to destabilize when they hit, tumbling end over end as they travelled through the body, drastically increasing the wound effect: 'The hardiest soldier turned sick when he saw the effect of the pointed German bullet, which was apt to keyhole so that the little hole in the forehead where it entered often became a huge tear, the size of a man's fist, on the other side of the stricken man's head' (Hesketh-Prichard 2013: 26). In fairness, this was an inherent property due to the aerodynamic shape of the bullet, and the German round was actually less likely to do this than the British .303in round, where the effect was deliberately magnified by packing the hollow nose with lightweight material; Ernst Jünger complained that 'British bullets with their brittle points are dumdum by any other name' (Jünger 2003: 53).

This soldier has tied his skis together to create an improvised shooting rest for his Kar 98k. (Tom Laemlein/Armor Plate Press)

TOTAL KAR 98K PRODUCTION 1934–39

Manufacturer	Pre 1940 code*	1934	1935	1936	1937	1938	1939
Mauser Oberndorf	S/42, 42	15,737	182,317	256,367	256,312	251,606	279,078
JP Sauer & Sohn	S/147, 147	7,656	75,574	198,514	178,458	180,413	199,259
Erfurter Maschinenfabrik (ERMA)	S/27, 27		3,456	23,347	99,265	168,339	135,709
Mauser Borsigwalde	S/243, 243		7,671	35,077	80,889	176,308	237,661
Berlin-Lübecker Maschinenfabrik	S/237, 237			11,452	46,180	84,692	118,780
Berlin-Suhler Waffen-und Fahrzeugwerke	BSW**				23,780	49,359	58,817
Gustloff Werke	337						9,295
Steyr-Daimler-Puch AG	660						17,426
Waffen Werke Brünn, Bystrica	dou						
Waffen Werke Brünn, Brünn	dot, swp						
Total		23,393	269,018	524,757	684,884	910,717	1,056,025

*Codes were used to identify manufacturers on most German military equipment, to hinder Allied intelligence. The codes used were changed in 1940, though some plants did not switch over until 1941 and some manufacturers were assigned two codes. Early rifles use a suffix to the code to indicate year. 1934 was 'K', and 1935 was 'G'. From 1936 on, the year was shown.

**Uniquely, BSW is not a code but the initials of the plant, and is the only one to appear in upper-case letters.

As an anonymous World War I German deserter reveals in *Unquiet Fronts*, however, some soldiers did modify their ammunition for greater lethality, regardless of the rules of war and the fact that men captured carrying such illegally modified ammunition were often shot out of hand:

> They are manufactured by the soldiers themselves. If the point is filed or cut off a German infantry bullet, so that the nickel case is cut through and the lead core is laid bare, the bullet explodes when striking or penetrating an object. Should a man be hit in the upper arm by such a projectile the latter, by its explosive force, can mangle the arm to such an extent that it only hangs by a piece of skin. (Anon 2013: 125)

The SmK round (*Spitzgeschoß mit Kern*, or 'Spitzer with Core') was a steel-cored armour-piercing round, originally developed for use against snipers' armoured loopholes but rapidly pressed into service against the first tanks. A later and much less common variant – the SmK(H) (*Spitzgeschoß mit Hartkern*, or 'Spitzer with hard core') – had a tungsten-carbide core instead of steel.

German blank ammunition usually featured a wooden bullet, rather than simply a crimped case, and the Wehrmacht used it extensively during training, believing that it made exercises more realistic. When Allied troops captured examples of these blank rounds, rumours started that the Germans were using wooden bullets because they wouldn't show up on X-rays, making it harder to treat wounded men. In fact, these 'bullets' disintegrated when fired, and were only dangerous within a few metres of the muzzle.

The B-Patrone (*Beobachtungs-Patrone*, or 'Observation Cartridge') incorporated a phosphorus incendiary element, and a small explosive

TOTAL KAR 98K PRODUCTION 1940–45								
Manufacturer	Post-1940 code	1940	1941	1942	1943	1944	1945	Total 1934–45
Mauser Oberndorf	byf, svw	415,457	336,441	380,421	1,142,336	1,434,219	205,591	5,155,882
JP Sauer & Sohn	ce	215,188	210,592	183,321	326,535	207,289		1,982,799
Erfurter Maschinenfabrik (ERMA)	ax	131,274	93,799					655,189
Mauser Borsigwalde	ar	198,211	121,802	110,489	120,652			1,088,760
Berlin-Lübecker Maschinenfabrik	duv	196,534	179,291	242,402				879,331
Berlin-Suhler Waffen-und Fahrzeugwerke	BSW							131,956
Gustloff Werke	bcd	130,144	163,669	158,188	315,107	348,081	91,679	1,216,163
Steyr-Daimler-Puch AG	bnz	130,492	109,714	117,836	217,880	175,816	196,625	965,789
Waffen Werke Brünn, Bystrica				95,582	409,502	408,636	29,712	943,432
Waffen Werke Brünn, Brünn	dot, swp				219,843	621,959	187,684	1,029,486
Total		1,417,300	1,215,308	1,288,239	2,751,855	3,196,000	711,291	14,048,787

pellet that exploded on contact with any surface. Although designed as a target-marking round, it was sometimes used by snipers and inflicted horrific wounds. Due to their slightly unstable explosive filling, B-Patrone rounds had to be carried and stored with some care. Although using such ammunition against personnel violated the Hague Conventions, its use was permitted for snipers in 1945 after a decision approved by Hitler personally – but only on the Eastern Front.

Shortage of materials forced the Germans to experiment with steel (rather than brass) cartridge cases during both world wars, but good quality control meant that German ammunition was generally very reliable, even after storage under poor conditions in the field.

IMPACT ON WAR PRODUCTION

An important aspect of the Mauser rifles' impact was the sheer number produced. Even looking purely at those produced for the German military, and ignoring the tens of millions made in other countries, the totals are impressive. Exact manufacturing figures for World War I are difficult to obtain, since many of the original documents are lost, and figures for issues to units do not distinguish between newly manufactured weapons and repaired ones. However, the best figures suggest that the German Army had 2,273,080 98-series rifles and carbines in stock at the outbreak of war, and another 7,221,312 were produced between then and November 1918.

Before 1914, the Gew 98 was manufactured by the Prussian state arsenals at Spandau, Danzig and Erfurt, the Bavarian arsenal at Amberg, and the Mauser and DWM companies. With the need for increased war production, they were joined by additional manufacturers: Schilling, Haenel, Sauer & Sohn, Simson and Oberspree. Numerous measures to

Two female workers posing with a 'shooting machine' used to test sight alignment, probably at the Mauser factory at Oberndorf. The joint Mauser/Zeiss machine allowed a task that had previously required a trained marksman to be done by unskilled workers, provided they followed the steps correctly. The author is not able to explain why the machine appears to have been set up outdoors. (Tom Laemlein/Armor Plate Press)

increase production were put in place, including night shifts and the employment of women to replace male workers called up for military service. As well as manufacture at rifle factories, some rifles were assembled from components manufactured by a number of decentralized factories, which were brought together for final assembly. These weapons were marked with a five-pointed star (and are hence known as 'star rifles'). However, the main production bottlenecks were on components such as receivers, which could not be produced by this method, and the programme did not increase production as much as had been hoped. Supplies of new weapons were augmented by systematic recovery of weapons lost on the battlefield. Troops were paid a two-mark bonus for each weapon recovered, and these were then sent to the rear for repair, reconditioning and re-issue; by 1917, such 'recycled' weapons made up a third of weapons issued to new troops.

After World War I, the state arsenals were liquidated, and the small Simson company became the sole supplier for the modest number of new rifles needed by the Reichswehr. During World War II, production was undertaken by a number of private industrial firms, and ultimately captured plants in occupied countries. Individual factories were identified by code letters, to conceal total production numbers, but the overall best estimate is that total production of the Kar 98k between 1934 and 1945 amounted to some 14,048,787 weapons.

Although the Kar 98k required numerous machining operations to precise tolerances, experience and the various simplifications to the weapon reduced the average time to produce each Kar 98k from 25 hours at the start of World War II to as low as 16 hours by July 1944, though plants varied in efficiency; this figure would have fallen even further with the additional simplifications of the *Kriegsmodell* version. Despite the improved productivity, shortage of labour meant that the factories employed not just women, but conscripted labourers from the occupied territories; at the Mauser plant at Oberndorf, the latter formed 55 per cent of the workforce by July 1944. In addition to the main factories, many other companies were employed as subcontractors – FN in occupied Belgium produced large numbers of bolts and barrels, and even concentration-camp labour was used to produce parts.

Total production of 98-series weapons for Germany alone totalled 23,543,181 weapons between 1898 and 1945. For comparison, the M1 Garand was the standard US rifle throughout World War II and the Korean War, and 5,468,172 were produced between 1936 and 1956. Prices varied between years and contracts, but 55 Reichsmarks – the average World War II price for a Mauser-produced Kar 98k – may be taken as the lower end. Price comparisons are difficult, but this equates to roughly $22 or £5 10s in 1940 (somewhat less than the $26 or £6 10s an M1 Garand cost), or the equivalent of $360 or £235 at the time of writing.

CONCLUSION

The Mauser Gew 98 and its descendants were among the most influential rifles of the 20th century. They set standards for ruggedness and reliability, and remained the equal of any other rifle available until the appearance of the Soviet and US self-loaders 40 years later. Mauser provided the main German infantry weapon through the greatest conflicts of the 20th century, and the huge numbers produced by Germany alone completely

A Waffen-SS soldier in Normandy. Although no longer cutting-edge technology by 1944, the Kar 98k was still a lethal weapon in the hands of a trained soldier. (Cody Images)

A Waffen-SS soldier on the Eastern Front cleans his Kar 98k while his exhausted comrades sleep. Note that he has completely removed the bolt to clean it thoroughly; although Mauser rifles were rugged weapons, grit and dust would still cause them to jam. (Cody Images)

dwarfed the production of any other rifle in either of the world wars. Even these enormous figures represent only the tip of the iceberg. Whereas none of the other world war-era rifles, such as the Lebel or Lee-Enfield, achieved any meaningful sales to foreign armies, the Mauser achieved a level of ubiquity not seen until the appearance of the Kalashnikov series. While this book has inevitably concentrated on Mauser rifles in German service, the huge numbers produced for other countries should not be forgotten. At one point or another, more than half the countries in the world issued Mauser rifles, and an estimated total of 100 million were manufactured worldwide.

The Mauser adapted to new circumstances, with shorter weapons replacing the original Gew 98 when the latter provided unwieldy in the trenches. It was adapted to new roles by adding telescopic sights or grenade launchers, and served reliably on battlefields from the South African veldt to northern Norway, and from China to Cuba. However, technology and tactics evolved constantly. The Mauser had ruled the battlefield when first introduced, as the 2nd Anglo-Boer and Spanish–American wars showed. Improved artillery and machine guns pushed it into a subordinate role, though it remained the most common German personal weapon until the end of World War II. Its extremely solid design meant that wartime examples still turned up in the colonial wars of the 1950s and 1960s, and on into the Balkan conflicts of the 1990s. Tens of thousands are still going strong as sporting rifles, half a century after they were made. Whether the criteria used is historical importance, technical excellence or number produced, the Mauser 98-series weapons must be among the most significant rifles of the 20th century.

BIBLIOGRAPHY

Anonymous & Feldwebel C– (2013). *Unquiet Fronts: Two personal accounts of German soldiers during the First World War.* London: Leonaur.

Ball, R.W.D. (2011). *Mauser Military Rifles of the World.* Iola, WI: Gun Digest Books.

Bidermann, Gottlob Herbert (2000). *In Deadly Combat: A German soldier's memoir of the Eastern Front.* Lawrence, KA: University Press of Kansas.

Duffy, Christopher (2006). *Through German Eyes.* London: Phoenix.

Götz, Hans-Dieter (1990). *German Military Rifles & Machine Pistols.* Atglen, PA: Schiffer.

Hesketh-Prichard, H. (2013). *Sniping In France.* London: Leonaur (originally 1920).

Holmes, Richard (1994). *Firing Line.* London: Pimlico (originally published as *Acts of War: The Behaviour of Men in Battle* in 1985).

Jünger, Ernst (2003). *Storm of Steel.* Harmondsworth: Penguin (originally 1920).

Law, Richard D. (1993). *Backbone of the Wehrmacht: The German K98k Rifle 1934–1945.* Ontario: Collector Grade Publications.

Law, Richard D. (1996). *Sniper Variations of the German K98k Rifle.* Ontario: Collector Grade Publications.

Lubbeck, William (2006). *At Leningrad's Gates: The story of a soldier with Army Group North.* Newbury: Casemate.

Olson, Ludwig (2002). *Mauser Bolt Rifles.* Montezuma, IO: F. Brownell & Son.

Orwell, George (1989). *Homage to Catalonia.* Harmondsworth: Penguin (originally 1938).

Pegler, Martin (2004). *Out of Nowhere: A history of the military sniper.* Oxford: Osprey.

Pöppel, Martin (2008). *Heaven and Hell: The war diary of a German paratrooper.* Stroud: Spellmount.

Reibart, Dr W. (2010). *Der Dienstunterricht im Heere* ('The Service Instruction in the Army') translated by John Baum. Lisbon, OH: www.GermanManuals.com (originally 1943).

Reitz, Deneys (2010). *God Does Not Forget: The story of a Boer War commando.* Tucson, AZ: Fireship Press (originally 1929).

Senich, Peter R. (1982). *The German Sniper 1914–1945,* Boulder, CO: Paladin Press.

Storz, Dieter (2006) *M98 Rifle & Carbine.* Vienna: Verlag Militaria.

Ulrich, Bernd & Ziemann, Benjamin (2010). *German Soldiers in the Great War: Letters and eyewitness accounts.* Barnsley: Pen & Sword.

Wacker, Albrecht (2005). *Sniper on the Eastern Front: The memoirs of Sepp Allerberger, Knights Cross.* Barnsley: Pen & Sword.

Walter, John (1976). *The German Bayonet.* London: Arms & Armour.

Walter, John (1979). *The German Rifle.* London: Arms & Armour.

Westman, Stephen (1968). *Surgeon with the Kaiser's Army.* London: William Kimber & Co.

INDEX

Figures in **bold** refer to illustrations.